W9-BMG-612

CONFESSIONS

of a

GERIATRIC

PROM QUEEN

Lila Lee Silvern

Copyright © 2014 Lila Lee Silvern. All rights reserved. No part of this book may be reproduced in any manner or form or by any means, electronic or mechanical, including photocopying, recording, or by any information storage and retrieval system, without the written permission of the publisher — except by a reviewer who may quote brief passages for magazines, newspapers and Internet sites. The cover of this book may be shown on the Internet or in promoting the book elsewhere.First Printing 2014.

Although the author and publisher have made every effort to ensure the accuracy and completeness of information contained in this book, we assume no responsibility for errors, inaccuracies, omissions, or any inconsistencies herein. Any slights of people, places or organizations are unintentional.

Library of Congress cataloging-in-Publications Data

ISBN 978-0-6159-9031-6
Printed in United States of America

For information contact: Random Harvest Press
lilaleesilvern@att.net

Cover Concept:	Raul Montes
Cover Design:	Maria Meehan
Author Photo:	Nancee Lewis

Acknowledgments

My thanks to:

Beverly Mickens and the story tellers at the Story Salon in Studio City, California.

Writers at the monthly meeting of Independent Writers of Southern California (IWOSC), the West San Fernando Valley satellite group.

Teachers in writing classes.

Raul Montes for his cover concept.

Maria Meehan for her cover design.

Sylvia Cary for her encouragement, editing, and publishing consulting.

Friends who have not only inspired some of these stories, but have also generously read them, or listened to me read them, and have offered critiques on them.

Proof-reading help from: Ethel Golub, Linda Parker, Dr. Stephen Sobel, Ellen Switkes, Jeri Vargas, Nancy Cott, Lee Gale Gruen, Judith Allen and Curtis Danning.

Computer help from my very patient tech assistant, Rebecca Leach.

Special appreciation to Noreen Stone for her encouragement to publish the stories and the time she spent reading and editing the book twice.

I especially want to express my appreciation to the man who is my Saturday night swain and still makes me feel like a prom queen, as well to those who have passed — but will always hold a special place in my heart and in my memory.

I've changed some of their names and taken dramatic license to enhance, exaggerate, and extract the humor from real life's most ordinary situations.

Dedication

To the love of my life, Eric, my son, who has always encouraged me to live life to the fullest and enjoy every moment.

Introduction

Confessions of a Geriatric Prom Queen

When I told my friends I was writing a book about senior sex, they thought I meant a book for high school seniors. "Not exactly," I blushed and went on to explain that my true romance stories were about men and women past sixty. They were surprised. They giggled with embarrassment at first and then couldn't suppress their curiosity about older people like their parents, grandparents, and me, yearning for love and romance in our senior years.

It seems to be the last taboo in film and TV. These days we think nothing of seeing mixed races or gay and lesbian couples making love, but when was the last time you saw two older people enjoying sex?

My stories are culled from my own experiences and those I hear in beauty salons and from friends over whispered lunches and in the women's locker room of the YMCA.

A 78-year-old widow friend told me while we were doing chair exercises how she was asked out by a friend who had known her since high school.

She expressed all the excitement and anxieties a twenty-year-old might have about going to bed with him. Her glowing face and wide smile at the gym a week later told us she was into a hot and heavy romance, which gave all of the jealous sixty and seventy-year-olds something to look forward to. Love is a young emotion, at whatever age it's felt. Sexual satisfaction might involve a little more patience and creativity and help from the gynecologist and urologist. The sense of little time to waste when one is older means no time for inhibitions and fears to get in the way of pleasure. No kids, no birth control pills, no work demands to keep you from enjoying a glass of wine, soft jazz from the iPod and a little late afternoon lovemaking. No need to wait until Saturday night. He can be younger. She can be overweight.

The most important ingredient isn't Viagra and vaginal lubricant, but a robust sense of humor, no matter your age or gender, whether you're involved in a sexual activity or reading these stories. I have included a few pre-sixty romances which were fraught with more inhibitions and expectations than the freedom felt in my later years feeling like a prom queen enjoying the attention of elderly courtly gentlemen or the playfulness of some younger "dudes" in their early seventies.

Lila Lee Silvern
Sherman Oaks, California — 2014

Contents

Online

I'd love to tell my friends I'm dating Mark Twain.
They'd admire my high-tech ingenuity
when I tell them I met him online.
A Silicon Valley dude clones history's
most dateable men for discriminating women.
I pressed the app for Sam Clemens,
sent him my resume, bio, and photos,
cropped and artfully recreating me at thirty-nine.
He must have liked what he saw on his iPhone
because he texted me in his original handwriting
(worth a mil)
and suggested we rendezvous not in what
I expected, a replica of a riverboat at Disneyland.
No, he suggested a bar in a downtown hotel
where he could smoke a cigar.
It smelled of old wood and leather, whiskey, and
Cuban tobacco. So did he.
I needed to know whether to call him Sam or Mark
or Mr. Clemens.
"All the same to me," he said, munching on some
nuts with salt that sprinkled on his wrinkled white
suit and moustache.
I sipped my julep and waited for him to reminisce
about Tom, Huck, and jumping frogs at Calaveras.
But all he wanted to talk about was his dead wife.
like any other widower I'd met in present life.
I waited for him to make me giggle and blush
and even put the hand that held his famous pen
upon my knee
but all he seemed to want from me
was the same as most other elderly gents I know,
admiration and sympathy.

Dinner for Four

I love to eat. I especially love being invited to dinner on a first date. Coffee is fine for college kids and still young forty-year olds, a Jamba Juice for high schoolers, but for late bloomers and geriatric prom queens like me who aren't yet ready for the early bird meal, an evening of dining is preferred.

There have been five significant men in my life since my divorce many years ago. Each one will be forever remembered for the restaurants we enjoyed in his geographical part of Los Angeles.

Señor Don Juan entered my life in a warm-up suit on an Encino tennis court, in the upscale area of the San Fernando Valley, the day my husband moved out. Don liked to move fast whether it was flying a plane, riding his Harley, galloping on a horse, or capturing the heart of a new woman. When we first met, his idea of a good meal was a T-bone steak or spare ribs at Monty's, a popular restaurant for carnivores. At the peak of our romance, to prove his adoration, he was ordering filet of sole with a few spinach leaves at a seafood restaurant on the same boulevard.

I did reconnect him with his Latino roots, and fondly recall drinking Margaritas at Casa Vega while mariachis serenaded us with Las Mañanitas, on Rosh Hashanah, the Jewish New Year. When the romance began to spoil like last week's crab legs, he yelled at me, *Yo no voy a comer otra vez una ensalada de salmon, nunca jamas en mi vida.* He would never eat another salmon salad for the rest of his life. He left my bedroom and returned directly to his carnality and a booth at Monty's Steak House. Still, for all the good enchiladas we enjoyed together, to honor his *memoria,* I avoid all the Mexican restaurants west of Sepulveda Boulevard.

Mr. Johnny Walker-on-the-Rocks was my Studio City, North Hollywood guy for a lot of years. He ran a sheltered workshop for mentally disordered sex offenders, which might explain his need for alcohol. He was a Jewish/Irish New Yorker with a tough, street-wise exterior and a heart of gold. I ate. He drank. We danced, laughed and smoked a lot of his cigarettes in trendy bistros east of Sepulveda.

On-the-Rocks had a few drinks before he got to my house, a few after and then a bottle of wine at dinner. While I satisfied my sensual cravings with chocolate mousse topped with whipped cream for dessert, he sipped an after-dinner Drambuie. He died of lung cancer and I gave up smoking, but not eating and dating.

Mr. Harvard U., the lawyer, writer, bon vivant, and political name dropper, came into my life shortly after his wife died and he moved into a beautiful high-ceilinged pad in West Hollywood, just south of Sunset.

We did Le Dome and Greenblatt's Deli on Sunset as well as those places that change names every two weeks. He always reserved a table for three, which I questioned, until I realized that way we weren't squeezed into a small table in the corner. Harvard had earned some early fame and a lot of money as a lawyer in a high-paying personal injury case. This enabled him to give up law and move to Mexico where he became a successful writer. When he returned to California, he dabbled in politics. Harvard walked into a room or a restaurant sure that everyone would know him and like him and vote for him.

He didn't look like a Prince Charming. He had a big nose, thinning hair, an even thinner body and very thick glasses, but when he opened his mouth and spoke, he was the most attractive man I'd ever met.

His eyesight was so bad he had to put the menu against his thick glasses to read it. He took off his glasses when he kissed me, and he thought I was the most beautiful woman in the restaurant. Harvard U loved women more than food.

He died peacefully in his sleep one night after take-out sushi at his place. I seldom eat in West Hollywood since his death, but of course, if someone did invite me to Le Dome, I'd tell him to reserve a table for three and lift my glass in a toast to good old Harvard.

Mr. Movie Maker was my all-time great love for six years. He was a retired actor-director who lived near many trendy Westside eateries. We met on a blind date. If I had been warned of his good looks and director credentials, I certainly wouldn't have dressed in beige and wouldn't have suggested a modest little Indian restaurant in the neighborhood. He insisted on driving me back to his more affluent side of Los Angeles and a charming Italian bistro where the romance started over veal scallopini and a fine bottle of wine. I was in my late fifties, but felt like twenty and acted sixteen.

I bought all new lingerie and purged my closet of beige.

Six months later, in that same restaurant, he stood up to join in an operatic duet with the owner and fell over, suffering the first symptom of Parkinson's.

We had a wonderful first two years when the medicines and all his body parts worked. We had another two years in the enchanted condo pretending he was going to get better. Our last meal together was served by his Filipino care giver who served the pizza delivered from Dominos. We watched an old movie my lover had been in when he was young and gorgeous. I rarely eat in his side of town now and when I do, it's always with a woman friend.

My current Saturday Night Suit lives in a luxurious condo and his favorite restaurants are in Beverly Hills. He is well past the age when my other lovers died, so I feel no need to warn him I could be lethal. When he called me the first time to invite me to dinner he asked, "Are there any foods you can't eat?"

I responded, "No, I eat everything in sight." He then assured me that he was still able to drive at night.

Saturday Night Suit, who always wears a tie if we are to dine, likes to be greeted with recognition by the maître'd, who is the only other man wearing a tie in the restaurant. He likes places that aren't noisy because he's hearing impaired, and if he leans in too close to hear me, his hearing aid goes off like a whistling tea kettle.

He likes to eat at a civilized eight o'clock, which is late for me, and is often my seventh meal of the day. By the time the server brings the menu, I feel like taking a chunk out of it but wait patiently, filling up on olive bread and tapenade while my date drinks his second scotch slowly. When we finish at about ten, I feel stuffed and drowsy from the rich food and wine and I am in no mood for affection or snuggling. I want to get home to my own bed and go to sleep. Lately, I've noticed Mr. Saturday night is moving the dining time up a little closer to six.

Now, I'm urging him to get a new hearing aid which might help the romance, because no matter our age "we women cannot live by olive bread alone." I've also enrolled in a CPR class just in case.

If the Shoe Doesn't Fit

After two months of Saturday night dinners, first run movies, and a play at the Music Center, E.J. invited me to his condo to see his etchings, original paintings, and Lladro collection. Our relationship was moving along rather slowly. We had a standing Saturday night date. Never on Sundays when he went to the cemetery to put flowers on the grave of his late wife, Evelyn.

"She may not have been perfect, but she was perfect for me," he repeated several times.

I pulled up to the gate of his impressive complex. I was permitted to enter after the attendant checked my name and license number and looked disdainfully at my Honda Civic in need of a wash.

E.J. greeted me at his door and extended his hand. I was about to shake it, but instead leaned into one of those hugs with no chest or breast touching. I was about to place a kiss next to his moustache, when a whistling alarm was set off. It was the sensor in his hearing device. Hearing impairment is a killer of romance and macular degeneration an enhancer.

E.J. led me into his condo as if he were conducting a tour. He did show me his etchings along with the Oriental screen selected by the interior decorator to compliment the white carpets, white sofa and matching chairs. I knew I could never bring my dogs there, and was a little fearful that I might have brought in a flea or two that would be easily detected.

E.J. was especially proud of the little china cabinet in the dining area. It displayed Evelyn's collection of crystal, china and Lladro purchased while on their many cruises around the world. There was a story to each piece which I heard that first evening and on several occasions since. Evelyn's presence was everywhere. There were photos of her on tables, credenzas, dressers and walls in every room. She was smiling on board ship wearing a beautiful gown and looking up at her beloved who was a lot taller and younger inside those picture frames. They were at weddings and office parties and in sunglasses and straw hats and Bermuda shorts lounging by pools in resorts in Hawaii and the Caribbean.

We moved from room to room with E.J. recalling those wonderful moments of his life with Evelyn. We finally reached the bedroom. I admired his custom-made bed spread and armoire. Then he took my hand in his and led me not to the bed but to a louvered door of a walk-in closet. He opened it with a flourish and it was as if I had suddenly entered Neiman Marcus after hours.

There, neatly arranged in a custom-designed closet were racks of Evelyn's skirts, pants, dresses, coats, blouses, and robes still in plastic garment bags since her death two years before.

E.J. proceeded to pull out leather jackets, cashmere sweaters, and new shoes, never worn, many of them still bearing the expensive price tags. He held up each item of clothing and checked the label, some of which I recognized and others from stores much too exclusive for someone on a teacher's salary.

E.J. loves labels. If I compliment him on a shirt or sweater, he always twists his neck and collar to reveal the Hilfiger or Polo label. If he shows me his Rolex or Seiko, I show him my Target. I was surprised when he invited me to try on Evelyn's clothes and take anything that fit. He didn't want the clothes to be worn by people who would not appreciate their value and his late wife's good taste in clothes as well as in men, he added with a smile.

There was a pair of $350 Ferragamo pumps, never worn, size seven. I wore seven and a half, but was determined to fit into them. I think at that moment I was prepared to have my left big toe amputated, if necessary.

"I'll have them stretched", I winced in pain.

There was a leather jacket, with sleeves a little too short and the wrong shade of brown; but I thought I don't have to button it, and maybe the tailor could add some contrasting leather cuffs and I could wear a bright colored scarf to cover the gap.

I secluded myself in the bathroom trying on pants that couldn't be zipped up and blouses that couldn't be buttoned, but anything with elastic in the waistband or of a knit material was modeled and set aside.

He placed the clothes that almost fit in neat garment bags and the sweaters and shoes in plastic bags. It was almost as if he were gift-wrapping them for me. I figured what I couldn't wear I'd give to friends or a charitable organization.

I wondered at first if he would be saddened to see me wearing Evelyn's clothes, or if he would be more upset if he didn't see the clothes on me. It didn't seem to matter. He liked me in her clothes or out of them. I've given away all the shoes that weren't open toed, even the $350 Ferragamos that cost $5 to be stretched.

No matter how many times I go to his condo, I still leave wearing or carrying something that belonged to Evelyn. I don't look anything like Evelyn. I'm taller, younger, weigh more and have different coloring. I've actually grown rather fond of the sweet departed lady, smiling happily from the photos.

I've almost emptied two of the closets. There's still one to go, and of course, the drawers and hey, what about the jewelry chest on the bureau? E.J. still goes to the cemetery with flowers, but not on the Sundays when we're enjoying a leisurely breakfast together.

The Enchanted Condo

I fell in love at fifty-eight. My neighbor arranged for me to meet Mark Harris, divorced, recently retired and open to meeting a new woman. I was divorced, still working and ready for a new man in my life. Without great expectations, after a series of disappointing blind dates, I dressed in drab beige pants and flat comfortable shoes. When I opened the door, my date smiled a friendly hello.

Oh my God! I could not believe the sudden pounding in my heart, sweaty arm pits, and oxidized tongue. I felt a hot flash come over me that was more pre-adolescent than post-menopausal. The friend who had introduced us told me he had worked in movies and television. She never mentioned his thick salt and pepper hair, blue-green eyes, black eyelashes, and square jaw. He looked like a model for a Cialis TV commercial.

When Mark asked me where I'd like to go to dinner, I suggested a modestly priced neighborhood Mexican restaurant. He countered with a trendy Italian bistro in his upscale neighborhood.

"That's so cool. I've wanted to eat there," I gushed like one of the teenagers in the ESL class I taught.

I was glad none of my feminist friends could hear me. What is happening to me, I thought as I grabbed my purse and followed him to his car, forgetting to turn on the burglar alarm and turn off the lights. I wished I were wearing something else, something I didn't even own but could have bought if I had known this blind date would be so damned good looking.

He opened the door to a shiny red sports car, and I clumsily lowered myself in.

"Oh no!" I gasped realizing I sat on his glasses. "I'm so sorry," I said, relieved that the lenses weren't broken, only the case.

For months afterwards he would joke, "Good thing I wasn't wearing them."

It was one of those glorious evenings that a woman past fifty-five doesn't think she'll ever experience. My escort was not only movie-star handsome, but he had a wonderful sense of humor, was modest about the shows he directed and was even interested in hearing about my boring life.

When I barely touched the veal and took only one spoonful of chocolate mousse, I knew I was falling in love. I was oblivious to everyone else in the room. I felt breathless the entire evening as we talked about our childhoods, our careers, our dissolved marriages, and our children.

It was a perfect evening. Mark's kiss goodnight was sweet and made me tingle. I was disappointed that he didn't press for more. That night I couldn't sleep. My heart and mind were racing; I was already replaying the dumb things I'd said about movie stars and the smart things I should have said about foreign films. I was sure that this handsome director who had been with beautiful actresses and starlets of film and TV would not be interested in a middle-aged school teacher who should have had those two chin hairs plucked.

He called two days later and invited me to see *Honey, I Shrunk the Kids* at the Director's Guild. It was the most surprisingly wonderful movie I had ever seen. I loved sitting next to Mark and hearing him laugh and feeling his hand on mine. For the next two months we went to movies and plays and usually ended up at his place in West Los Angeles. His condo looked like a movie set for a bachelor pad, furnished in antique pine and comfortable tweed upholstery with floor-to-ceiling bookcases filled with books on theatre and history, photos of famous movie people, a great sound system for jazz CDs and a king-sized bed where we spent most of our time.

Sometimes I would wake in the middle of the night and look at the man whose hairy muscular arm lay across my naked body, and I would think about all the rich and beautiful women who were living in condos just like this and sleeping alone or with men they didn't love. I wanted time to stand still. I dreaded the coming of morning when I'd have to get up and step out of a Technicolor musical to return to the reality of the gray inner city where I worked.

When I called the friend who had introduced us, all I could say over and over again was, "Wow, I really like him." A month later, Mark called to thank the same friends and to invite them to have dinner with us.

In the ladies room of the restaurant where we met, my friend squealed with delight, barely able to contain herself.

"I've never seen you both so happy. Mark needed someone sensible like you after all those glamorous airheads he dated."

That isn't exactly what I wanted to hear, but I still hugged her and we giggled like school girls as we returned to our table.

Mark stood up to pull out my chair and without any warning, he fell backwards and lay sprawled on the carpeted floor. The maître'd, waiters, and I bent over him. He looked up, shaken and embarrassed, but not seriously injured. We made light of it, attributing his fall to the wine and the poorly constructed chair.

The reality was that none of these things were to blame. It wasn't dizziness. It wasn't the first time. He promised me he'd see a doctor and find out what the problem was.

"Probably nothing," we assured each other.

A week after that dinner he was in his kitchen fixing his favorite spaghetti sauce. As he offered me a spoonful of the thick hot mixture he said, off-handedly, "I've been diagnosed with Parkinson's and I'll understand if you walk out the door."

"What?" I said, "and miss this great spaghetti dinner!"

I didn't know what Parkinson's was and even later after I had read the brochure, *Moving in the Slow Lane*, I still wasn't about to walk away from this man I adored.

That first year, with the medication, the symptoms eased and there seemed to be an improvement. He wasn't falling as often. His energy level improved. I was surprised when friends noticed the way he began to shuffle as he walked, the way his facial features seemed frozen, and that fact that his speech was slightly slurred.

I tried to disregard how hard it was to read his cramped writing on the cards tucked into the whimsical, wonderful gifts he wrapped for me on our first Christmas together.

We celebrated New Years at the condo with Taittingers champagne and caviar. I ruined the Cornish game hens that dried out in the oven while we were making love on the floor in front of the fireplace.

As the months passed, we began to spend more and more time in the condo where life was safer and easier for Mark. When we did leave to attend a party or a screening where his friends might be, I held onto him so he wouldn't lose his balance, and I did this in a way that masked his handicap and emphasized our closeness.

He was covered with bandaged cuts and black and blue bruises from frequent falls. I was less aware of the changes than his daughters.

They had no idea that the condo was enchanted. They didn't seem to notice that we hadn't changed from the way we were on our first date a few years before. In fact, it was as if we were regressing. I was twenty-one and Mark was twenty-six.

I was young and beautiful, the lines erased from my face, and he was healthy and handsome and sure footed. The smell of his Polo cologne disguised the smell of urine and stains on his clothes. We stored the furniture, broken from his falls in back of the closet. I was in denial, refusing to acknowledge what couldn't be hidden from his friends and family. One evening his daughter called to tell me that her father had been in another car accident. Fortunately, he and the driver of the other car weren't hurt, but the car was severely damaged. His daughter was arranging for a live-in assistant to drive and care for him.

She hadn't discussed this with either her father or with me. She behaved as if I were as impaired as her father was and an accomplice in covering up his true condition. Donny Mendoza moved in with Mark who resisted violently at first but eventually began to refer to him as "our son." I preferred to think of him as our chauffeur who drove us to screenings at the Academy on Wilshire while we cuddled affectionately in the back seat.

Friends no longer invited us to their homes. They were fearful he might fall and break something. We spent all our time in the Enchanted Condo. Donny and I would call out for Chinese food or pizza, ignoring his daughter's orders for less salt and sugar. Mark began sleeping more hours than he was awake.

I would finish work on Friday and rush over to spend the weekend with him. It might be 4:30 in the afternoon, and I would find him in his dark and shuttered bedroom asleep or watching old sitcoms on television. When he sensed me on his bed reaching over for a loving kiss and hug, his face would light up. I still loved to stroke his hairy chest. The Depends and deteriorating body were not turn offs. They just didn't exist.

Donny treated him as if he were an Alzheimers patient. His daughter was running his financial affairs and questioning his expenditures and the nutritional value of Chinese take-out. I still treated him as the virile, healthy man I had fallen in love with six years before. I still burned with jealousy when he received calls from other women who had been in his life. I was upset when he called me by his ex-wife's name.

He could still make me laugh and blush with a tender line.

"Hey, Ace," he'd tease, "Take off your overcoat," referring to the red silk night shirt from Victoria's Secret that he had given me the first night I slept over.

Friends urged me to date other people.

"After all, you aren't married to him. He's well taken care of. You don't owe him anything. He wouldn't be doing the same for you," they were sure to add.

I knew all that, but in the Enchanted Condo he was still virile and attractive, and I felt beautiful and desirable.

I worried that Donny would go back to the Philippines and that Mark's daughter would send her father off to the Home for Old Actors.

But they didn't have to. He died peacefully in his sleep one March night. The daughters handed me my red satin night shirt in a crumpled paper bag and told me the memorial would be at the ex-wife's house. They hired a bagpiper to play *Danny Boy* and served Chin Chin's Chinese chicken salad. I read this poem:

Growing Old in Hollywood
I saw my love in a new light
on an old video
last night.
He was in black and white back then
smoking a cigarette in a tuxedo
kissing his movie wife on camera
and looking like his son

would look today
if he had one.
I'm not jealous of the time
we missed together
in the first two acts of his glamorhood.
I didn't know him when
he was acting and directing
able to get in and out of a sports car
and performing with ease in all his parts.
I felt more comfortable
with him in the un-reel world
retiring to the enchanted condominium
we created.
I had no problem with
his shoulders a bit stooped
his hair a wiry gray
I liked him better that way

In Act III I let him direct
all the love scenes
we played together
in winter light and unmade up faces
touching, touching tender places
sharing insecurities,
growing old in Hollywood.

Fade Out

My lover left me in March, on my sixty-fourth birthday. I had been with him the night before and saw that he was suffering from a bad cold with the added complications of Parkinson's disease. I gave him a kiss on his forehead and left him in the care of Donny, his Filipino helper. I told him to get better so we could celebrate my birthday on the weekend. He died early that morning.

His two daughters had his ashes divided into four packages. One for each of them, one for his ex-wife of 20 years and one for me, his "lady friend" of six years.

One daughter scattered his ashes on the grounds of the movie studio where he started his film career. The other girl went to New York, to scatter hers near Broadway where he had acted on the stage and in television. The bitter ex-wife kept her share close to make sure he'd never leave her again.

Eleven months passed with the cylindrical carton of my late lover's ashes over the fireplace in my den squeezed in between the ashes of Basil, my loyal Doberman and Mouse, my beloved Dachshund. Sitting atop the smallest tin was an ornament of a wiener dog with halo and wings.

My response to those who questioned the lightness of the container was that in no way was it a measure of his manliness. There were those lewd snickers that inferred that I was given his lower part in lieu of money, real estate, and TV residuals.

After ten months of mourning and looking at the mantle crowded with ashes and covered with dust, I decided it was time to scatter my honey's remains and get on with my life. February 14 was the date I chose to free his ashes from the cardboard confines and set his soul free to make great movies in heaven. The place I chose was a beach near the Venice canals, close to Hollywood, not Rome. We had spent some happy days there in a borrowed beach condo two years before. He loved the sea. He was a sailor in World War II. He lived near the beach when he first divorced.

I called my friend, Joan, who owned the condo, to ask if I could park in her garage and use her bathroom, beach and VCR. I also called Nina, another friend who was a movie buff, romantic and available that morning.

There is a law that you cannot dispose of remains without a permit, but I figured that no one would be on the beach on that drizzly Valentine's Day when my friends met me in the condo garage. Nina always asks what she should wear, be it a cocktail party or ash scattering. I told her to wear warm beach clothes since we would be assembling close to the water on that dreary, February morning.

I was in sweats, rolled up to the knees, old tennis shoes and a waterproof jacket with a hood. Nina showed up in a tweed skirt, cashmere turtleneck, Burberry rain coat, a rather charming little hat and high heeled-boots. For those looking down on the beach from their window, they would have seen a curious party of four making their way down to the water. I led the procession carrying the round brown carton of ashes in one hand and some red carnations that I had bought at a nearby supermarket in the other. Joan in her orthopedically correct rainy day beach shoes and carrying a camera, was in front of her husband, Peter, who had a look on his face that said, *What am I doing down here when I could be home checking the stock market?* Trailing ten feet behind was Nina trying to keep up in her high- heeled boots.

We were the only people on the beach. I had to work fast before someone reported me for performing what I was prepared to say was a religious ritual. My three accomplices watched as I picked up a piece of driftwood, engraved a large heart in the wet sand and chanted a little bit of "Schma Israel" instead of "Funny Valentine" in case the shore patrol showed up.

I gave each of my friends a red carnation to toss into the heart or near it or somewhere in the sand. While Joan was busy snapping photos of the flowers strewn on the sand, I struggled to get the top off the container. With Peter's help I was finally able to pry it open. I could see in the distance a jogger approaching and a beach tractor coming from the other direction.

I held the carton in front of me and with a motion that resembled someone scattering bird seed, I slung my arm out towards the sea hoping to see a stream of ashes land in the wet heart. But just then a sudden wind from the west timed with the encroaching tide blocked the cascade of ashes so that they returned to my face and mouth just as the cold wet sea water flooded my heart and shoes and swept the carnations, driftwood, the cremation carton, and the heart outline out to Catalina and beyond.

"Oh, shit," I sputtered as Nina searched through her handbag for a tissue to wipe what was left of my beloved from my face. The tragic-comic scene needed some Nino Rota movie music. Where was Fellini when we needed his direction?

We trudged back to the condo to warm ourselves, eat bagels, drink coffee and watch the video I rented from Blockbuster. In it my lover was young and handsome and even his smile was different from that of the older man with Parkinson's who had spent those few days with me at the beach two years before. I remembered now how he resented the wheelchair we wanted him to sit in and how he struggled to go into the surf, but fell and Donny and I had to rescue him.

I know that he, as a director, would have approved of the gray dreary desolate beach, the sad heroine with the shabby clothes and wet feet, and Nina, her good friend who was the only one to include him at a dinner party. But he would definitely have said, "cut" to his last few years.

I shook my head dramatically posing for another one of Joan's photos, and noticed a smudge of ash that had fallen on the cream cheese of my half-eaten bagel. I bit into what was left of it and my life.

Another Part of the River

The Yuba River runs through the foothills of the Sierras, near the quaint old California gold rush town of Nevada City, where my cousin lives and would like me to move. For years, she has tried to entice me to leave the crime and smog of L.A. and join her in Paradise.

"But I couldn't live in a place where everyone is a massage therapist," I explain. "I would miss the ocean, ethnic foods and the better odds of meeting a single man in a big city."

Then, a few summers ago, she called all excited like a prospector who had just discovered gold near her property. She found me a bachelor who lived a mile down the road before you got to the sewage dump.

Two weeks later on a hot July afternoon, I wheeled my suitcase into her guest room and freshened up to meet Edward Chapman for tea at his place. Chaps, as he liked to be called, greeted us at the door. He was tall and thin and very tan. His hair was Grecian Formula tan also. He had to be in his early 80s, judging by the World War II medals hanging on the wall.

He served tea and the pound cake he had just baked, all the while chatting about his wonderful childhood in England and his adventurous move to Australia to work as a forest ranger. After two hours of tea and a tour of his small, neat house, he asked me, "Would you like to accompany me to the Yuba River tomorrow?"

"That would be wonderful," my cousin answered. "She'd love to."

Chaps arrived punctually in his vintage Volvo and put my beach bag next to two towels and a walking stick he had carved for me. As he drove over the bumpy road, he very casually asked me if I had ever been to "this kind of bathing area before." Carefully choosing his words, he informed me as a tour guide might, that the beaches along this part of the river are "clothing optional."

"You mean nudist beaches?" I blurted. "I don't think my cousin knew."

Chaps reassured me that it was optional.

"You don't have to remove your clothing if you don't want to. If this is not comfortable for you," he added, sensing my shock, pursed lips, and clenched fist, "we could go to another place on the river right off the highway." He slowed the car down looking for a place to make a U-turn.

"No," I stopped him. "Don't turn around. I've been to that beach where people go with their babies and grandparents. This time I want to see another part of the river."

With great excitement, he gunned the engine and we went bumping over the dirt road that took us to a clearing where he parked. "Now, you know," he addressed me before opening his door and running around to let me out, "you don't have to take your clothes off if you don't want to."

I looked him directly in the eye and said, "I know that. Are you going to take your clothes off?"

"I always do," he answered with a wink.

I smiled, offering some hope.

He escorted me a down a steep path to the river. When we reached the narrow beach, I was awed by the beauty of the scenery and a few sunbathers on rocks. They were bronze all over. Chaps placed the two towels on the sand. I sat stiffly on one, while he slowly unbuttoned his denim shirt. He sat beside me as he loosened his leather belt and explained his philosophy of nudity.

"You see," he said, in his clipped British accent, "whenever clothing touches your skin, a message is sent to your brain making you aware of the contact and distracting you from higher-level thoughts. Now that I do not feel the collar and cuffs of my shirt against my body, my mind is freer."

Hoping for the same enlightenment, I pulled off my T-shirt. Then I reached around and unhooked the bra that I realized was binding my breasts and as Chaps explained, my brain and creative output. He had already taken off his jeans and was now pulling down his jockey shorts which he folded and placed neatly on the rock behind him. I pulled off my shorts and Costco panties and placed them next to Chaps' undergarments on the same rock.

I turned modestly as he stood up, all six-feet-one inch in front of me, and I couldn't help but notice that he had a long uncircumcised penis and instead of pubic hair, a scar, which he explained was from a hernia operation. He had continued shaving that area of his body ever since. Mine was not to question why. Mine was but to do or die. I took out a tube of sun tan lotion and Chaps offered to do my back. I did my front.

I looked around to see if anyone was watching us. No one was. I moved away from my hiding place next to the boulder and stretched out on the towel. Chaps sat down on the towel next to me, but not too close. Even our towels didn't touch.

Then I removed my final covering, sunglasses, and looking directly at him, confessed to how little I knew about England and Englishmen. From that moment, 11:37 A.M. until three hours later, Chaps recited the entire unabridged history of the British Empire, including all the Anglos, Saxons, Goths, Teutons, Kings and Queens that ever appeared in a text book read by a British school boy.

I began to worry that I might be tested. I excused myself a few times to cool off in the refreshing river. Chaps stood, watching and waving to me and keeping track of exactly where he left off, so that he could continue when I emerged.

The warm sun and Chaps' history lecture made me sleepy. It would have been nice to shut my eyes and doze off, which I did a few times, without his even noticing. We were finally into the 20th Century and approaching World War II, in which Chaps had served as a Royal Grenadier. It was almost four and we were getting close to the Battle of Monte Casino. More of the locals were arriving and shedding their work clothes. It was getting harder to concentrate on the valiant efforts of the British infantry when there were so many interesting bodies to look at.

He stopped after D-Day and we packed up to leave.

Chaps was right. As soon as I started to put my panties on, I felt the elastic pinching and biting my skin. My bra felt like a leather harness so I put it in my bag instead of over my slightly rosy breasts. No need to weigh my mind down with too many straps and too much spandex.

Chaps did not seem tired or thirsty or in need of a loo after his all-day seminar on the glories of Great Britain. He was so exhilarated and pleased with my company that on the way back, he invited me to his home that night for dinner. I accepted and then wondered what I should or shouldn't wear and whether I dare ask about the flora and fauna of Australia.

I'm not planning on moving to Nevada City, but I am wearing fewer underclothes.

Goodbye Mr. Chaps

It was a chilly October afternoon in Nevada City as I parked my car in Chaps' driveway overlooking Deer Creek. I always recognized the house by the varnished red sign at the side of the road.

> Chapman's Old English Tavern
> Bitters-Lager-Ale-Scrumpy
> Tea served 3-5
> Snug Lodging
> (Ladies *only* please)

Chaps met me at the door fully clothed in a long sleeved sport shirt and jeans. On my last summer visit, as I approached his house, I could see him on the deck watering his plants. He had greeted me then with nothing on but a smile and a wink.

The first time I had seen his long, lanky body bare of hair and underwear was when he introduced me to the Yuba River and the benefits of nudity. I had also seen him looking very distinguished, clothed in a tweed jacket with suede elbows, when we went to the local art show. I can still hear his lively voice as we walked the dark quiet streets of Grass Valley and he chanted loudly:

"There was a young man from Divizes
Whose balls were two different sizes.
One was so small.
It was no ball at all.
And the other so large it won prizes."

It must have been a limerick he remembered from his days as a Royal Grenadier in Her Majesty's army. He had complete recall of every battle, especially the Battle of Monte Casino, which he had recounted to me on several occasions. He had saved many of the news clippings, documents and photos from his four years of service. He loved to show me the one of him as a young blond lad looking very handsome in his spiffy uniform.

Chaps was still nice looking in his 80s, even though a little stoop-shouldered, and the thick blond hair of his youth was now a thin pale brown that he claimed was natural. His bifocals magnified his blue eyes. Peter O'Toole could have played Chaps as an old man; Gary Cooper when he was younger.

I had called the day before to tell him I was in town for a few days.

"Thrilled to hear your voice," he answered, sounding very sincere and eager to see me.

The excitement continued as he busily brewed tea and sliced his freshly baked pound cake. I watched as he poured the hot water over the tea and covered the tea pot with a wool cozy he knit himself. After all, he built all of his own furniture with hand tools he brought from England. He described himself as the kind of man who could shear the sheep, spin the wool, weave the fabric and tailor the suit or knit a sweater or a cozy.

He moved about his kitchen chatting nonstop about his son, now living in New York, his cat, now in heaven, and his trip from England to Australia when he was sixteen. He realized even at that young age that being the son of working-class parents, he didn't have a very promising future in England. He jumped at the opportunity to have his passage paid to Australia where he would work for the forestry service. He was assigned a job in the remote outback where for a year, he and another man hiked 500 miles surveying the uncharted landscape. I pictured him in Bermuda shorts and a pith helmet. That's where he learned about forests, timber, animal life and aborigines.

He returned to England at the outbreak of World War II, enlisted in the Royal Grenadiers and survived the most hard-fought battles in Africa and Italy.

"Please pass the sugar."

I hated to interrupt. He hardly touched his tea. His face was flushed as he went on to tell me how he got to Brazil after the war. Now I imagined him in a wrinkled white linen suit applying for a job in a British importing company and actually getting the job because an employee with the same name had died the week before and there was a vacant desk and name plate waiting for him.

"I'll have another piece of cake, if you don't mind."

Without a pause he continued to describe his adventures as he sliced the pound cake and then brought out pictures and news clippings from a dusty old box.

I carefully wiped the cake crumbs from my fingers before looking at the photos he showed so proudly which I had seen on previous visits.

"I'm waiting to hear about romance in Rio de Janeiro," I teased him.

He rolled his eyes. "Oh, the women were magnificent. Can I get you some more tea?"

I shook my head, no, realizing I had stayed longer than I had planned. My cousin would be expecting me back for dinner, I explained. He looked terribly disappointed.

"Maybe I can get back tomorrow before I leave," I said.

He walked me to my car. I thanked him for the wonderful stories and the great tea, and reached up to give him a friendly hug goodbye. He responded with an unexpectedly long and passionate embrace. When he finally released me, he put his well-worn and elegant hands inside my jacket and squeezed both of my breasts affectionately.

I pulled back with surprise. Then we both laughed uproariously, our faces red, his blue eyes twinkling behind his bifocals. He directed my car out of the driveway so I wouldn't go into a tree or down the ravine and into the creek.

I'm sorry I didn't get back the next day to hear the rest of his story.

My cousin called last week and told me that Chaps died shortly after my visit. I am sure that I was the last woman who listened so attentively to his life story and brought him some measure of carnal delight.

I learned from my dear friend, Chaps, about the role of the British army in the battles of Italy, the knowledge obtained from reading the *Economist*, the joys and delights of swimming naked in a warm river and the pleasure of a freshly brewed cup of tea and a slice of homemade pound cake eaten with a charming and distinguished Royal Grenadier.

Goodbye, Mr. Chaps. I'll miss you.

Love in the Time of Chanukah

I will always remember my first Christmas as a fourth grade teacher at an elementary school in Pacoima, a barrio north of Los Angeles. It was the year I dissolved my marriage of 17 years, got a teaching job and met Ricardo Caraballo on a tennis court, the day my husband moved out.

After having been married to a red-haired beauty queen and a blond Olympic diving champion, Ricardo was charmed by my lack of fame. I was an almost middle-aged substitute teacher with no seniority, who was desperate to learn Spanish so I wouldn't be transferred to a school in South Central Los Angeles.

I was the first to volunteer for everything, including the Holiday Breakfast and the Winter Festival. Of course I would direct the Posadas, even though I had no idea what it was.

It seemed I was more interested in succeeding in my new job as an ESL teacher than I was in romance or a second marriage. I took Spanish and Chicano Studies classes at night, watched Mexican novellas on Channel 34 and read *La Opinion*. On weekends, *mi amor* gave me wonderful lessons in colloquial Spanish, how to drink tequila like a Yucatan native, and advanced love making.

I drove him crazy, not with sex, but with *"como se dice?"* this and *"como se dice?"* that. The poor man couldn't eat a meal without my asking how do you say artichoke dip or gefilte fish en *Español*? When we were making love, which was a lot of our time together, I had to know *la palabra* for every part of my body and his, and still had a problem using the familiar *tu* form of the verb to describe our very intimate relationship.

We talked every school night on the phone. He said I was beginning to sound less Chinese when I spoke Spanish and more like Yolanda, the fourth-grader who was going to play Mary in the play. I noticed that *she* was beginning to sound more like me, spitting and high pitched.

I would hardly have been noticed as the new teacher if it hadn't been for Ricardo riding into the school parking lot on his Yamaha to pick me up for a quick *lonche* on *Lankerchim*. The window blinds of the teachers' lunchroom would part as my nosey colleagues watched us speed off.

During lunch I shared my little classroom dramas and disappointments. After one week of intensive English, Joel came into the class saying, *"Chut up chut up!"* which I never taught him. He had such a loud voice that I cast him as Joseph in the Posadas.

I asked Ricardo to help me pronounce the name of a new student who got so tired of correcting the way I said *Gerardo*, he finally said, *"Yust call me Yerry."*

I did Chanukah with my class and with Ricardo, who at this point said, "Just call me Richard." The potato latkes tasted like hash browns and he had as much of a problem with *"l'chaim"* as I had with Gerardo.

Richard suggested I try his mother's recipe for *chile rellenos* instead of latkes, and he helped me make them for the holiday breakfast. They were way too spicy and a little runny, but the auditorium was so dark I don't think anyone noticed. Tables with red cloths, festive decorations and candlelight were set up in the space below the stage. The hall was transformed into what looked like a night club at seven in the morning.

Everyone dressed up for the event. The organizers had been working since six in the morning. Some were high on caffeine. Others were high on the bourbon and brandy being secretively added to their coffee.

I got there early and greeted the parents with a smiley *"orale"* just as I had heard the guys in my Chicano Studies class say. Ana Maria, my teaching assistant whispered, "We don't use that expression. It's *Pachuco.*"

I was undaunted. I eagerly went over to greet the President of the P.T.A., Gloria Garcia. She was a petite woman with dark hair down to her waist, a creamy complexion and very large brown eyes outlined with black eyeliner and mascara. She was wearing a velvet jacket and on the lapel was a sparkly seasonal ornament. I looked at her adorable pin and said, "What a cute little *chingadera* you're wearing."

Señora Garcia gasped in shock. Her creamy complexion turned *roja*. Her large eyes opened even wider. Ana Maria shook her head in disbelief.

"Doesn't it mean thingamajig?" I stammered apologetically. "Mi amigo, Ricardo, he always says, *Chispa,* give me *la chinga*...when he's ..."

I only remember her enormous eyes widening in disbelief and my conversation with Ricardo that evening telling him how embarrassed I was to have said "little fucker" to the P.T.A. President.

That wasn't the end of my teaching career, but it may have been the beginning of the end of my relationship with Ricardo Caraballo. What started out sweet as flan, was souring fast. He began to tire of the old Mexican melodramas I dragged him to at the Million Dollar Theatre downtown. He was also getting a little jealous of all the time I spent at school and my devotion to my students.

When we broke up for the fourth time and I was very depressed, I decided to write him a letter -- in Spanish. Between sobs I wrote,

Mi Querido Ricardo,
     I am writing to you to *expresar mis emociones.* If only you could have been more sensitive..." Hmmm could have been. That sounds like the conditional subjunctive. Should I use *hubiera* or *deberia* or *tuviera*? "If you had not been such a *pendejo, chingadera."*

I realized that our relationship had always been a rather subjunctive one, filled with possibility, and always uncertainty.

Not a Christmas passes when I don't see some cute little ornament affixed to someone's lapel and want to smile and say, "What a cute little *chinga-majig* they're wearing."

Feliz Navidad, wherever you are now, Ricardo Caraballo, Gloria Garcia, and you, too, Yerry.

I Left My Heart at the Buena Vista

It was a cold wintery night in November, long before smart phones, when my best friend and I made our way to the Buena Vista Saloon. We had just spent a very boring day at the *La Literatura Infantil* Conference in a big, drafty, old hotel in downtown San Francisco.

Charlotte and I had registered for this very esoteric gathering just so we could get away from our work as bilingual teachers and also distance ourselves from recently ended romances. We practiced our Spanish whenever we were together until we halted over a subjunctive verb translation describing the lovers we were trying to forget.

"If only Ricardo had been honest with me," I lamented.

"If only Bert hadn't told me he would leave his wife," Charlotte snapped.

She was even more depressed than I was.

A little woman who looked like Ayn Rand with thick glasses, chain smoked in front of an almost empty hotel ballroom extolling the benefits of reading to children from Spanish literature books. I was falling asleep.

Charlotte leaned in to wake me and said, "Let's get out of here and go to the Buena Vista for a drink and some shopping at Cost Plus. The drink sounded good. We made our way to the cable car five pounds heavier in layers of our warmest clothes, hats, gloves, and scarves.

We arrived at the famous little Saloon just north of Fisherman's Wharf. It was four-thirty on a Friday afternoon, and every seat at the bar was taken. We waited at the door until a gentleman towards the back of the narrow aisle stood up and beckoned to us as if he and his friend were about to leave. The stool he vacated was still warm. I looked up to thank him and was dazzled by his smile. His teeth were as white as his starched shirt, and he smelled of an expensive cologne and British cigarettes. He had the look of a movie hero with slicked down hair and a well-tailored Brooks Brothers suit. I began to heat up immediately, and he was kind enough to help me off with the first layer of coat and scarf.

He introduced himself and his friend who offered his seat to Charlotte. I ordered a sherry. My new friend requested that the bartender bring me a Harvey Bristol Cream.

I caught a glimpse of myself in a mirror behind the bar. My cheeks were flushed and I was glowing even before the first drink. I removed my gloves. Roger was very attentive. He wanted to know what brought me to San Francisco and all about my work as a teacher. He told me he was also a tourist from nearby Oakland, here at a dental convention. Two other drinkers left and he was able to sit and order another round of drinks. I felt the hot flashes of menopause and this attractive gentleman dispelling the gloom of a cold night in San Francisco. I was down to my skirt and blouse and pearls.

I had wolfed down my third sherry and consumed all the nuts on the bar when Roger came up with a wonderful idea. He suggested that we all go tea dancing at the Hyatt. He stepped over to his friend, Jim, who was on the other side of Charlotte, and included them in the invitation. I looked over at Charlotte who was looking at her watch.

"Charlotte, we've been invited to go tea dancing at the Hyatt," I beamed, expecting her to beam back. She moved over to the seat next to me, still bundled up in most of her layers.

"Tea dancing at the Hyatt!" I repeated.

"I heard you the first time," she said. "*You* were invited, not me."

"Of course, Roger meant for the four of us to go," I explained.

"I don't think Jim really wants to go with me," she said.

"Of course he does," I whispered. "How could any man resist your charms?"

"He reminds me of Bert, and I thought we had plans to go to Cost Plus," she said, her lower lip quivering.

"We can go tomorrow afternoon before our flight back," I pleaded.

"You go dancing, if you want to. I'll take the cable car back," she said with such sadness in her sometimes beautiful face that I realized I was faced with a major dilemma.

Should I go off with this man of my dreams and leave my depressed best friend to cry herself to sleep and be a bitch for months after, or go with her to Cost Plus at Fisherman's Wharf for a bowl of thick pasty clam chowder and a meander through a store that held no charm for me.

I opted for the latter. That was in the late seventies, a long time ago. I've replayed the scene many times, enticing Charlotte to the ladies room and getting on my knees to beg her to come, or offering her money or telling her I would die if I couldn't have one dance with my dream man.

When Charlotte died of cancer, I finally almost forgave her. But I never forgot what might have been.

Take Two

Milton called from Best Buy, all excited. "Baby, have I got a surprise for you," he said in his sexiest voice. "I finally bought it. You are going to love my new Sony, DCR 108 Camcorder with 40X optical zoom. Put on something really sexy. I'm coming by to try it out on you."

I felt very lucky to have a man in my life who turned me on with his knowledge of megabytes, megahertz, Blackberries, iPods, iPhones, Kindles, Nooks and what they could do to make our lives more youthful.

I tore off my gray work-out sweats and jumped in the shower. Like a speeded-up old movie, I washed my hair, shaved my legs, dusted myself with powder, smeared myself with lotion and sprayed myself with White Diamonds cologne.

I put on a new black lace nightie and cut off the Victoria's Secret tag, size L. Over it, I draped a sheer, slightly faded negligee I pulled from the bottom drawer of my still-hopeful chest.

The door chimes rang. I smeared pale gloss over my lips and blush over my cheeks. I slipped into strappy high-heeled sandals and almost tripped on the negligee as I rushed to open the door. There stood

Milton, the 68-year-old short and stocky Romeo I had met at a senior center zumba class. He swept me into a warm and passionate embrace which I hoped would not mess my hair or makeup before the "shoot."

I gently pushed him back and reminded him of the package he was still holding in his hand. Flushed and embarrassed by his senior memory moment, he laughingly reminded me of how my proximity was always a distraction.

Milton carefully withdrew the little digital video camera from its box and directed me to assume a sexy position on the sofa while he read the manual and made the necessary adjustments on his new toy.

"We are about to make our own jerk-off flick," he joked with a mischievous glint in his eyes.

I hated his crudeness sometimes, but at that moment I, too, giggled at the thought of posing for an adult film rather than a newsletter for retired school teachers' pension plans.

Before "assuming a position" I hobbled to the mantle to remove the pictures of my children and grandchildren from the background of the movie we were about to create. Milton called me back with, "Lights, camera, action!"

Posing seductively, shyly at first, I felt self-conscious and awkward with Milton's directions to caress my left breast with my right hand and stroke my inner thigh with my left hand. He led me on with suggestive encouragement, while I kept reminding him to get my better profile and not focus on a varicose vein or bunion.

After a few more hot words and suggestions from Milton Von Stroheim to relax and let go, I began to imagine myself as one of those sexy lingerie models or the heroine of a bodice-ripper gothic romance. I was just getting to the point of a moan or a whimper or a breathless piece of improvised dialogue when I was derailed with "Cut! Do you want to see what I've got, baby?"

"I know what you've got," I snapped impatiently at *scenus interruptis.*

Milton was fooling around with the camera and obviously pleased with what he saw. I sat up and peered over his shoulder, curious to see myself on the tiny screen.

"I think I need a magnifier," I said, squinting as I stumbled about on high heels looking for my glasses. Milton read the directions on how to hook the camera up to the TV so we could see it on the big screen.

"Hey, doll," he called to me. "Come see yourself on X-rated TV."

I came back, barefoot and wearing my bifocals. I sat down next to Milton who was fiddling with the remote.

"I told you I'd make you a stah, dahlink," he pronounced in a fake accent that still sounded like Brooklyn.

I watched, fascinated from the sofa where a few minutes before I had been posing and contorting and playing an exotic sex symbol. At first I didn't recognize the image I saw in very High Definition on the 52-inch flat screen. I thought that the makeup would have covered the dark puffiness under my eyes and the lines around my mouth. The hair was not a flattering silver but a rather dull pewter.

Worst of all, whose body was that in lingerie that didn't fit? What was that skin doing hanging from my thighs and upper arms? And the breasts, so saggy even lying down. I gasped, "Turn it off, Milton. I don't want to see any more. It's a horror film."

"You look great, sugar. You're turning me on," he said, trying to convince me.

I had hoped I would feel like Claudette Colbert in a Preston Sturges screwball comedy circa 1930s.

What was missing was that wonderful soft lighting and expertise of a cameraman, as skilled then as a plastic surgeon is today.

"Turn it off!" I insisted hoarsely diverting my eyes from the screen and reaching for the remote in his hand.

He thought I was playing, and he teased me by holding it where I couldn't reach it. I went to the TV and found the power switch and angrily pulled the cord from the camera.

The screen went black. I ran to the bathroom, slamming the door behind me. Shaking, I ripped off the satin and lace, throwing them to the floor. I pulled the sweat suit from the hamper, desperate to cover my entire body with something warm, protective and concealing. I had gone from the heat of a tropical island to the North Pole in less than ten minutes.

Milton was at the door, tapping lightly and asking if I was alright.

"What went wrong?" he wanted to know. "You looked great."

"You should be scheduled for cataract surgery," I advised.

Milton didn't answer. I had hurt his feelings. I heard him in the living room packing up his equipment and getting ready to leave. I sat on the side of my bathtub staring at the puddle of pink and black lingerie on the floor. I saw my face in the mirror, advertising pension plans and losing my swing-dance partner.

I moved cautiously to the door and poked my head out calling to him, "Hey, Mr. Von Stroheim, are you ready?"

"For what?" he said, shaking his head in disbelief.

"Take two," I announced.

He grinned, "No close-ups, I promise."

"And no damn fucking bifocals," I promised, tossing my glasses on my sweat suit and slipping back into my slightly wrinkled negligee. "Lights, camera, action!" I laughed, moistening my lips and shifting to my best side.

Date Night

Dating in one's senior years can be different from teenage, young adult, and middle-age romance. There are the concerns about night driving, digestive limitations, hearing aid problems and other more personal romantic challenges.

There are a lot of changes from the sexy seventies to the not-so-naughty nineties. Here is the scenario I have come to expect with my elderly gentleman friend who is very proud to have turned ninety, announcing it to every waitress, ticket taker, parking valet, maitre'd, and stranger sitting next to us at a restaurant.

Our Saturday night date is usually an early movie, dinner, and coffee, dessert and maybe a game of Scrabble afterwards at my house.

When he comes to pick me up, he quickly finds a place to sit to catch his breath from the walk from his car, and then begins the stroking and petting and words to match in his still-sexy deep voice,

"Hello, doll baby. You are so gorgeous tonight. I've never felt like this for any babe before I met you, Mol."

My name isn't Mol. That's my dog, who is returning his affection with kisses and pawing, and a covering of blond dog fur all over his black cashmere jacket. He looks ashamedly at me across the table and into my eyes and repeats that Mol is "the only dog I've ever loved."

I should be happy that my Saturday night date no longer complains about dog hair on his clothes and almost being knocked down when he comes in. I am frankly jealous, though. He never talks to me that way. I've been seeing him on Saturday nights since he was a spry septuagenarian. Now he is an elderly gentleman who finds it difficult to walk, hard to hear, and the need to pee and cough up phlegm on a more regular basis.

The unsinkable Molly Brown is truly more beautiful and exotic than I. When I rescued her from the shelter they identified her as Korean Jindo, but since then her breeding has been guessed at by everyone we meet on our walks. People have stopped to offer their opinion of her antecedents, everything from Akita to Chihuahua on steroids. Maybe Basenji mix, but she doesn't bark and she's bigger. One vet was sure she was Shibu Inu Pit Bull mix. She is a well-built curvy 45 pounds. She has the posture of an Asian dog statue and beautiful dark eyes that look rimmed with eye liner. She loves to lie on her back and spread her legs to have her tummy rubbed.

Many times E.J. enters with a copy of the *L.A. Times* Sunday crossword puzzle he completed in ink in 30 minutes, knowing I'm still struggling with pencil and eraser. He sometimes presents me with a bottle of wine. I know that he goes to visit his late wife at the cemetery every Sunday and I once asked if he brings her flowers. He said he did. Then I asked why he didn't give me flowers. He said that next time he would bring me the carnations and take the Kendall Jackson to the cemetery. That shut me up.

I used to ask him if he wanted to drink some of the scotch which he left at my house. A Johnny Walker used to be a sure indicator of sexual activity a little later in the evening. Now it indicates to me that I should do the driving.

E.J. is a very courtly gentleman. It wasn't easy for him to accept my offer to drive to the movies. He still insists on opening the car door, even if it is on the street side with oncoming traffic or in a tight parking where we have a problem both squeezing into the narrow space.

He also insists on paying for the movie, popcorn, and dinner afterwards, which I accept with a gracious thank you and a kiss on the cheek at the end of the evening.

When we were younger and returned to my house after a movie, I would offer him something sweet and chocolate or me, but with the passage of time and bodily afflictions and diets, I now lead him to a cozy corner in the den with a fire in the fireplace and good lamplight. I bring out the big box with a well-worn, grown-up adult game. Scrabble. Yes, those little square tiles and that board that spins has now replaced sex, but isn't always safe when emotions are aroused.

The electronic Scrabble dictionary and the big Webster's sit beside us on the table like the vaginal jelly used to. We take turns putting our hands into the little burgundy bag filled with warm, smooth tiles. We finger them like foreplay, feeling a little surge as we draw them out and look at what we're starting with. There's a flirtatious, "guess what I have?" in E.J.'s manner, before he exposes his *P* and expects that I may show an *A*, but I don't. I have a *V* which means he'll make the first move. I'll have to respond.

He complains at the start that he has too many vowels and can't move them. I whine about my low scoring consonants needing some strong vowels to activate.

He starts with *A.E.R.I.E.* which is a rather esoteric show-off word to begin and flaunt his male dominance. All I can do with my lousy letters is place *T.* under his I to form *I.T.* which he extends and scores by changing it to *TITULAR*.

I am the scorekeeper. I'm so busy adding that I don't see him sneak down next to my *RACY* putting his *RAUNCHY* into a triple corner giving him 48 points. We move on and my heart begins to pound when I pull out a *Q*. I still have the *U* and I could form *EQUIP*. I just need to find a place to put it. I found it, but he takes my spot, and I get very angry. I tell him I hate him and he doesn't seem to care that he's being so sadistic. All he cares about is the damn scoring and being on top of his game.

I finally find a cheap place to dazzle him with my *EQUIP*, and the bastard has the nerve to add a *MENT* and claims it as his *EQUIPMENT,* scoring with my 10 point *Q*.

Now we are both getting hot. I have to turn the thermostat down and fill our glasses with Pellegrino. Oh, my heart is pounding. I'm feeling wet all over. I get a *Z* to make *QUIZ* which gives me double word points. Our scores are almost even with that move.

I look over at him. He has that impassioned look of concentration behind his glasses. He keeps reaching for the electronic dictionary which has replaced the vibrator in our relationship.

I slide my hand into the bag and pull out the *S* I've been praying for. Yes, I have a seven-point word that could earn fifty points. I just have to find a place to put *CONDOMS*. My head is throbbing. I feel about to explode. It's E.J.s turn. He scans the board.

"What can he be up to? Oh no, not there, don't go there, please, not yet."

He moves to the other side. I scream with ecstasy. I can get my seven point winning *CONDOMS* in a safe place where I can get 65 points and win the game. Oh no, I didn't make the right moves. I can only fit in the *CONDOM*. No room for my *S*.

E.J. surprises me with the letters to make it *CONDOMINIUM*. I add my *S* and wait for E.J. to challenge me. He doesn't. He's exhausted and lets me win.

I know he will consider it a Valentine's gift to me or he will say "Well, you had the *Q*."

And I would answer, "But you had the *Z* and the blanks." I think he let me win because he knows I'm a sore loser who pouts and whines and looks frustrated and unrequited when losing. There just doesn't seem to be a way we can come together in the end. As I give him his hug and kiss at the door, I worry that he won't want to play with me again unless I let him win the next time. No matter the decade, century, or our age, some of us women just can't stop playing games.

Brace Yourself

Some women bare their souls or their bodies. I'm about to bare my teeth, so brace yourself. I have two secrets to share. One is that I have been wearing braces on my teeth for a year and a half. And two is that I'm madly in love with my orthodontist.

Our liaison started when I casually mentioned to my dental hygienist on a day when I was feeling particularly old and tired and my teeth were looking very beige, that I was thinking of a face lift or getting my eyes done.

Her reply was, "You look great. Why bother with plastic surgery? What I would suggest is that you get your teeth whitened and a new pair of glasses." She placed a hand mirror in front of my mouth and added, "And maybe you want to see about getting that front tooth pushed back."

Oh my God, she was right. It looked like the giant front tooth on Fran's dragon puppet, Ollie. Why hadn't I noticed? The lower teeth were crowded together. The upper fang pushed out causing a separation. I would never smile or open my mouth again except to scream.

She had a coupon to offer for the whitening and an orthodontist's referral for the front tooth. Dr. B. turned out to be a man my age, semi-retired with salt and pepper hair, curly eyelashes, and a very nice smile.

He stared into my mouth. "Beautiful. Really gorgeous," he breathed heavily. I felt a warm blush come over me, until he called over his assistant to admire the gold crowns my dear departed dentist brother made for me when I was seventeen.

Then he asked if I knew about my "torus platinus." Not even my most ardent lover or gynecologist knew about this rare, bony protrusion on the roof of my palette. This was like our little secret, and explained my gagging at the slightest intrusion. I was more "Shallow Throat" than Deep.

I was told I'd need to get a complete set of orthodontic X-rays and plaster casts from a very high tech dental X-ray lab. The first surprise was lying down for one of the procedures. The large piece of equipment photographed the inside of my mouth and jaw from every angle possible. I had photos taken of me smiling, lips pulled back, profile and frontal. Fortunately the only thing I had to take off was my lipstick.

I returned to Dr. B the next week to view the unflattering photos, X-rays and plaster cast of my upper and lower teeth. He told me I would need wire braces on the bottom for a year and a plastic splint on the uppers. My insurance plan would pay for part of it. The cost would be affordable. It was a bargain compared to a face or eye lift. But still, I had to consider whether it was a good investment at my age. How would all the hardware affect airport detectors and my love life? Would the braces affect kissing, especially kissing someone wearing dentures? Would my phone message reveal my bilateral lisp? I decided to go through with it.

I scheduled the appointment to have the metal apparatus installed. When Doctor B finished clamping and wiring, I looked at myself in a mirror. I felt betrayed. The braces made me look like an aged adolescent with wrinkles instead of acne. And the damn things hurt. I was given instructions about applying strips of paraffin and brushing and flossing and not eating bagels, beef jerky, and Almond Rocca.

For the first week, the only advantage I saw in this silly idea was that the pain in my mouth and the scratched and bleeding gums definitely curtailed my eating. This was turning out to be a wonderful diet plan.

People immediately noticed the braces and wondered why I was wearing them since no one recalled the protruding front tooth that I thought had been so unsightly. The first week I considered having them removed but wasn't ready to end my budding relationship with Dr. B. so prematurely. I loved having his gloved fingers in my mouth, his masked face practically touching my nose and inhaling his intoxicating blend of Lavoris mouthwash and Polo after shave.

When I got bored reading *Boys' Life*, *Calling All Teens* and *Parent Magazine* in the waiting room, I brought in my own copy of *More* and *AARP*. I began to chat with the pimply faced adolescent in the next chair who was wearing a head apparatus that looked like a torture device.

Norm, which is what I began to call my orthodontist, opened up more with each visit. At last he had a mature patient he could talk to about tennis, the stock market, politics, arthritis and retirement.

The metal braces came off in one year as he promised, and my bottom teeth were in alignment like the stars, though not as twinkly. But, alas, Norm said the splints didn't work on my upper teeth and he would need to put braces on them, but the invisible kind that would cost extra. He just wanted my teeth to look perfect, or maybe he just hated saying goodbye. It would only be another few months, he assured me. The Invisalign braces are just as bothersome. They collect lettuce, chicken and cheerios. I never leave the house without toothpicks and floss.

I see Norm almost every week for some kind of adjustment or repair. When he told me they might come off in a few weeks, I got very excited. It would be like an unveiling of his work of art. He said we ought to go out for a beer afterward to celebrate, but I suggested corn on the cob instead.

Of course, I'm planning on rechecks and retainers.

Early Bird Catches the Worm

I was sound asleep when the phone rang. I thought I was dreaming, so I didn't open my eyes. Then I heard my cell phone chiming in from my purse on the dining room table. I opened one eye and glanced at the blue-lit clock. It was 11:30 p.m.

The ringing from the hallway persisted until my recorded greeting answered, "Hi. This is 818-727-5555. Please leave a message and I'll call you back." Then came the beep followed by a familiar, deep-night voice that whispered, "Just calling to wish you sweet dreams, baby, and tell you I love you. Are you there?" Then a second, even more plaintive, "Are you home?"

I didn't want to answer the phone. I needed to sleep, but I knew there would be another call. It came at exactly 11:40. I didn't answer. My purse in the dining room was about to join in. Then again I heard his soft, pleading, late-night voice asking me to pick up the phone or call him back on his cell phone when I got home.

I realized this might go on all night, so I rolled over to pick up the phone, and almost crushed my bed partner, Juan Carlos, a handsome ten-pound Chihuahua-mix.

"I can't talk. I have someone in bed with me."

I hoped that would blow every transistor in his Blackberry.

But he laughed, "Tell Juanito I miss him, too."

I was too sleepy to lie convincingly or to be clever. He knew me and my schedules: Sunday night, watch Masterpiece Theatre; Monday, fold laundry, pay bills; Wednesday night, Book Club; Saturday night, movie and dinner with a date.

He'd known me for a long-time. We used to work together. He'd been my friend and colleague many years before he wanted to be my lover, after my long-time partner's death. I appreciated his calls at first. He left messages in dialects that made me laugh. His sweet and loving words eased my loneliness. No matter what time of the day or night, I welcomed his call. I was angry when he didn't call. I was pleased when he did.

Now, ten years and ten minutes later, things have changed. My eyes are open at last. I tell him not to call me. He should be in bed with his wife. "Where is she?" I ask.

"On the other line," he jokes.

"That's not funny," I say.

"It is annoying," he laughs. "Just called to see how your phone is working."

It's the phone he gave me as a gift, trying to seduce me with upgraded technology. He's younger and really into electronic toys. I'm older. I like new shoes better than new phones, computers and younger married men. He's a night owl. He wore horn-rimmed glasses when I first met him. Now he wears contacts and needs cataract surgery.

"I told you not to call me after nine. I'm a morning bird. I get up very early to greet the dawn and I need eight hours of sleep."

"You told me not to call you ever," he said. "But I don't believe you."

"Believe me. I'm going to hang up and go back to sleep."

I do that. The phone rings again. After the message, I try to stop his voice, but instead I press something that blasts it over a loud speaker that I'm sure will wake the neighborhood. I have to get out of bed and trudge down the cold hall barefoot to push things to stop it.

Juan Carlos follows me and scratches the door to go out. I open the door and the alarm that I forgot to disengage goes off. I'm waiting for my hot, fiery fury to set off the smoke detector.

I hear Night Owl's voice hooting instructions on how to control my wayward systems.

There is a call-waiting beep. The alarm company wants to know if I'm O.K. I put Night Owl on hold while I tell them I am. I let Juan Carlos in. I forget that Night Owl is on hold and make my way back to bed with the phone in hand. Just as I am about to put it back into its cradle and rock it to sleep, it rings again. I pick it up.

"I just couldn't sleep," Owl whispers. "I kept thinking of you and missing you. Are you still as sexy as ever?"

"No, I'm not," I start to stage whisper and then realize I don't have to. "There isn't a husband sleeping down the hall in another bedroom," I scream at him.

Poor Juan Carlos looks at me and rubs his paw over his ear.

"Are you wearing that sexy purple nightgown I gave you for Valentines Day?" he wants to know.

"No, I'm in Costco flannel pajamas with gravity defying anti-wrinkle cream all over my face."

"I don't care how you look. I wish I could hug you and taste you." he whispers.

I tell him I can't hear him. Maybe I'm getting deaf. He tells me again what he wishes he were doing which I can't repeat.

"I'm wearing my Invisilign braces with teeth whitening jell. Tastes terrible. Go hug your wife."

He ignores what I said. "I just wish I could hold you. I wish I could feel your magic fingers on me. I'd even settle for a phone hug."

The phone makes beeping noises again like some kind of censoring signal.

"Is that your vibrator?" he asks. "The one I gave you at Christmas?"

"No, it's the lousy, cheap telephone you gave me for my birthday."

It is now 12:15.

"You sound irritated." he says. "Maybe this isn't a good time to talk."

"No time is good to talk, but especially night time. I'm an unmarried early bird. You're a married night owl. We live in different nests."

More phone static and piercing signals.

"This is ridiculous. I'm too old for this."

"You're ageless," he says.

"I'm not! You're just blind and deaf and conjugally deprived," I say to turn him off. "Goodnight. No kiss. No hugs. Just so long. It's been swell knowing you."

I hang up the phone.

I did not fall asleep for another three hours. I was filled with angry, dark, dramatic night thoughts. I played out farewell scenes. I composed final letters. I took an Ambien and still was awakened at 6:30 with pawing from Juan Carlos who needed to go out.

I greeted the dawn with a few yoga-style stretches and fresh-squeezed orange juice. I dressed, read the paper, drank coffee but instead of going to the computer to send Night Owl a message on his Hot Mail, I went to the telephone to deliver the message to his-and-her answering machine.

It was 6:30 AM. I did something I had never done before. I dialed his home number. It rang and rang and rang until the message came on. After the beep, I whispered in my sweetest, sexiest, morning voice, "Dearest Owl, just calling to wish you sweet day dreams, after our wild, wonderful, last night together. Are you there? Are you there?"

Slam. Click.

Moral: Early Bird Catches the Worm.

One Afternoon I Had Self Esteem

In my earlier years, I suffered from an assortment of paralyzing neuroses: agoraphobia, claustrophobia, freeway phobia, chronic back pain, migraines and a very shitty marriage to a math teacher who liked to give me math tests in supermarkets.

"Compare the price of these four rolls of toilet paper that are on sale with the six rolls on the shelf," he would demand.

I would break out in a sweat and begin dividing and multiplying on my palm. I failed every time and was getting sicker and less confident about ever being able to get better and be able to drive on the freeways or shop in a department store again.

Having lost weight, sleep and a lot of confidence, I was referred to Dr. Z., a distinguished psychiatrist who was gentle, kind, and a wonderful listener. He prescribed Valium and scheduled appointments every Tuesday for three very tearful but therapeutic years, until I was strong enough to leave the house, drive to a lawyer and get a divorce.

I had been on my own for about six months and was really proud of the progress I had made getting my life back together. I was balancing a checkbook, shopping in a crowded supermarket, riding in elevators and on escalators, and almost ready to drive on

Interstate 5. I had described it to the good doctor as the "Man's Freeway" with all those big trucks on my tail honking and puffing testosterone on my rear end. We all go through life with some form of a foot deformity, but some of us learn to cover up the limp better than others.

I really wanted to share my successes with Dr. Z. I started a few letters and thank you cards but never sent them. I wanted to see him, but not in his office where I had been a patient. I just needed to get up the nerve to call. I needed a sign from a higher power or an astrology chart.

The sign came to me one particularly beautiful morning. First, I read my horoscope in the *L.A. Times*. It said, "Your intuition is nudging you to tell someone your feelings. Don't hesitate. Trust your instincts and make the first move."

The second sign came like a religious epiphany when I pulled into a service station realizing that my gas tank was almost on empty. I was about to say my usual "two dollars please." But before I could, the station owner came over to the window and said, "There's a gas war on, lady. Gas hasn't been this cheap in years." I changed my mind.

"Fill 'er up," I proclaimed, and realized those were the high signs I needed to make the call that day to Dr. Z and ask him out for lunch.

I called him five minutes before the hour and his next patient. He was surprised to hear from me. "I'm doing well," I told him. "I'm doing very well. I'd like to meet you for lunch and tell you all about it."

"I don't usually go out to lunch," he stammered professionally, rather taken aback by my invitation. "But...." there was a long pause as he checked his calendar and finally came up with a date for the next week and a meeting place I could get to without driving on the 405 freeway.

I was so excited and nervous about seeing him outside his office that I had a recurrence of anxiety symptoms. What to wear? What to wear? I changed from beige to red and back to rather pale gray. I wasn't completely cured. My hair looked so drab and plain and stuck out like I had just had a shock treatment. I made an appointment at a fashionable salon to get it styled before I met him. I took a Valium to calm my racing heart and panic attack.

As I sat nervously waiting in the salon, suffering from menopausal hot flashes, a very attractive woman who appeared to be one of the steady customers was just leaving. Her platinum blonde hair was freshly coiffed in the bouffant style popular at the time. Her long nails were a striking shade of fuchsia with her lips a matching color. She looked glamorous and sophisticated in a perfectly tailored short wool skirt and high white boots. She looked like a movie star. She smelled of Virginia Slim cigarettes, Arpege cologne and Revlon hair spray. I was sure she was off to lunch with a producer or director at the Polo Lounge in the Beverly Hills Hotel.

I stared glumly in the mirror and felt very drab as the hairdresser gave me the quickie standard boyish bob that looked nothing like the chic page boy I had described. I was beginning to think this lunch was a big mistake. Maybe I should have gone to his office as a patient returning to have the psychoanalytic stitches and staples removed. Maybe I should have just sent a thank you card. No, I had to go through with it with the plain hair style and the smudgy glasses and the fingernails with the nail polish peeled off in nervousness.

Dr. Z. was waiting near the entrance of the restaurant, a few blocks from his medical building. He looked shorter away from his office and a little older, but very attractive with the thin moustache, graying temples, horn rimmed glasses and tweed jacket.

We were led to a leather booth, in a room fashionable at the time when people drank scotch and ate steak at restaurants owned by former football players.

"Well, how are you doing?" he asked in his wonderfully deep, soothing, sexy voice.

He lit a cigarette.

"A little nervous, Dr. Freud," I answered about to recline on the couch-like seat. Before I could, we were handed menus and asked if we'd like anything from the bar. The voice was waitressy, but the smell wasn't. I whiffed. I sniffed. It was Virginia Slims, Arpege and Revlon hair spray. The fingers holding the order pad were tipped bright fuchsia. I looked up.

Even in the dim romantic light of the restaurant, I recognized her. She hadn't gone to the Polo Lounge for cocktails after all. She was serving them instead at the Ram's Horn. I was the lady in subtle soft beige with the natural windblown hair sitting across from the elegant gentleman in the fashionable restaurant about to order a Chardonnay and throw away the Valium.

He insisted on paying for that lunch and all the other Tuesday lunches we enjoyed for many years. That afternoon was worth a year of therapy. And as for my self-esteem, it soared as did my spirits. You could hardly notice the limp as I left the restaurant.

Two Gentlemen from Bagdad

It was in the bar at the Biltmore Hotel, where I sat waiting for Lucretia to meet me after the last workshop of the Teachers of English TESOL Conference. It was a Friday night in the seventies, before we had cell phones. She was late as usual.

It would have been more fun to be staying at the hotel and partying that night. But the conference cost a lot and we were just glad to be able to leave our teaching jobs for two days. If I were alone in another city, I would have sat at the bar. I find that bartenders are especially attentive to teachers at conferences. My theory is that the second woman most men fall in love with, after their mother, is their teacher. Just tell the guy behind the bar that you're a fourth grade teacher and his eyes glaze over as he remembers that first infatuation with Miss Kelly, his fourth grade love. He usually fills your glass with a little more chardonnay and adds some nuts to the munchies and wants you to listen to his description of his beloved teacher. In my experience, men prefer teachers to blondes.

A gentleman who wasn't the bartender was staring at me from across the crowded room. He could probably tell I was a teacher because of all the books and junk stuffed into the TESOL bag on my table.

At the other end of the bar sat another woman, a blonde with only a large handbag, who looked like someone of another profession. He glanced her way and she smiled back. I suspected that neither one was there for the conference. His suit and tie looked Middle Eastern. He was dark complected with graying temples and very sexy eyes. He looked at the woman at the end of the bar again. Then he looked my way and lifted his glass.

I returned his smile. He took that as an invitation, and made his way toward my booth.

"May I join you?" he asked in a thick accented baritone.

He smelled delicious. I moved some of the books and papers aside so he could sit down. I asked him if he was attending the conference.

"No," he replied. "I am traveling as an assistant to a businessman from Bagdad whose English is very limited. I take care of all the travel plans and business arrangements."

"Your English is excellent," I told him. "I should know, since I teach English as a Second Language."

He put on his glasses and inspected the plastic identification card on my chest with great curiosity. He introduced himself as Kasim. I told him that I taught children from Mexico to speak English. I went on for several minutes until I noticed him glancing at the woman who had moved to a booth not far from ours.

"What is your work?" I said, getting his attention again.

"I was Chief of Police in Bagdad until I retired a year ago to become a personal assistant to Mahmoud."

"Assistant or bodyguard?" I wanted to know.

Kasim laughed at almost everything I said, which made me question his English language fluency.

"My travel companion is not a political leader. He is a very successful business man who owns the largest car factory in Bagdad and has interests in a shipping company." Kasim looked at his watch.

"He is resting now. Can I buy you another drink?"

He beckoned the waitress. I looked at my watch. "I'm waiting for my friend. She's probably busy shopping for her kindergartners."

"She has many children?" he asked.

"No, we're both teachers. She doesn't have any of her own children. She teaches kindergarten."

He took my left hand in his looking for a wedding band, and asked if my friend and I were married.

"Divorced," I told him. "And what about you and your friend? Are you married?" I asked.

"I have been married many years. My wife is a very old woman. She is 42."

I didn't tell him that I was only a few years younger and my friend, Lucretia, didn't consider herself aged at 45.

"Your wife must be very jealous of you traveling around the world without her and dealing with the temptations of school teachers in bars and saloons."

He laughed again.

"Jealous?" he proclaimed. "My wife is jealous of the water that touches my feet when I bathe. She is jealous of the shirt that touches my skin."

"Wow! That *is* jealous."

"And I cannot understand the husband that would leave so beautiful a woman as you." He said, looking over my entire body undressed and into my eyes behind my glasses. "You look like the kind of woman who should be wrapped."

Before I could ask him what he meant by that, he looked again at his watch and I looked at mine and we both spoke at the same time.

"I need to check on Mahmoud."

"I wonder where Lucretia is."

"Would you and your friend like to join us for dinner?" he asked, standing up and promising to return soon with Mahmoud.

As he walked out, Lucretia walked in carrying bags of teaching materials and looking exhausted. She was a tall blonde from South Dakota who had been married to a Latino and loved foreign men, but, I soon found out, not gentlemen from Bagdad.

"I have too many friends of the Jewish faith," she explained.

I thought for a moment and then assured her that every dollar spent on us for the evening would be one less for bombs for Israel and that we should be more tolerant of people of all religions and ethnicities, especially since we had been mandated to teach Multicultual Awareness. That was 1970-something.

When Mahmoud appeared, she changed her mind. He looked like Omar Sharif in a silk suit tailored in Paris with only one imperfection. His name was misspelled in the lining. He spoke very little English but had a beautiful smile. Kasim did all the talking.

Lucretia and I selected Bernard's, the most expensive restaurant in Los Angeles and just down the lobby from the bar. Lucretia, a woman of elegant taste, ordered the most expensive wine. Mahmoud and Kasim ordered scotch and Coca Cola. We realized that it had not been many years since their families had gotten off camels in the desert.

It was the first of several evenings the four of us spent together at lovely French bistros and Middle-Eastern cafes....as well as more intimate moments together.

Mahmoud and Lucretia did not listen to the advice Kasim and I gave freely about just enjoying this brief interlude together more as pen pals than lovers. They fell madly in love and continued their affair for several years. Lucretia finally realized she was never going to be a second wife in his harem. She married a man from Burbank she met in a square dance class.

Kasim told me on our last evening together that when he would be a very old man resting on his sofa and reflecting on his life, he would think of the time we spent together and remember me with great pleasure.

I thought of him when America waged war on Iraq, glad that he had probably not lived to see the destruction of his country, the automobile factory and shipyards.

Now that I am an older woman sitting at my computer reflecting on my past life, I often think of Kasim. It was many years ago, and I am still wondering as a woman and ESL teacher, when he said I looked like a woman who should be *wrapped*, did he mean in fur or raped? I'll never know.

Sick Happens

I woke at six in the morning with my head throbbing, my throat lined with sandpaper, and a cough that would have registered 6.2 on the Robitussin scale. Swallowing two Tylenol was the morning's accomplishment. Orange juice stung. Coffee was out of the question.

I bundled up in fleece to go outside and get the paper. That exhausted me. I climbed back into bed in my pajamas, a sweat shirt, a shawl and a robe. I realized I didn't really know how to be sick. I didn't have enough practice. I had taken care of many sick people in my lifetime, but who was left to take care of me now that I was really sick? I managed a few calls to cancel a dentist's appointment and a date with my Thursday sweat shirt, a youngish, techie friend who helps me with my computer, TV, ego and sex life. He was heartbroken, but understood.

I was disappointed that he understood. I felt old, sick, and alone, and realized that when I got my heating bill, I would also be poor. Where were my women friends when I needed them? I thought of sending out an email asking for volunteers to come over and sister me in this moment of need, but I couldn't leave the comfort of a warm bed for a cold computer.

Rrring..rrrring. Finally someone got my telepathic message. It was E.J., my distinguished, elderly Saturday suitor, making his weekend planning call. I croaked a barely audible, "Hello'.

His response was his usual cheery, "How are you?"

"Not so good," I coughed back.

"What? I can't hear you."

E.J. is hearing impaired and listening deficient, and I was having a problem getting any volume from my voice.

"I'm not well."

"What?"

" I'm really sick."

In the six years I'd known him, I'd never been really sick before. He offered to pick up a prescription and some cough drops at Rite Aid and a pizza and chopped salad from Maria's.

Just looking at the pizza made me sicker, which he couldn't understand because it was healthy vegetarian. He ate most of the pizza and salad while I sucked on Echinacea lozenges, coughed and slept through two black and white Turner Classic movies. Technicolor had gone out of my life.

Early the next morning, I got a phone call from the third man in my life, my theatre escort, Sidney. He called to notify me that his emails were being returned because of my full mail box. When I told him I was sick, he offered to bring champagne, caviar, vichyssoise, zinc, and Nyquil. He ended by telling me he would re-send the joke that had bounced back, sure that it would make me feel better, and that he would look for another well person to go to the theatre with him that night.

I staggered feverishly to the computer to delete MoveOn.org, Groupon, and Bloomingdales, and all of Sidney's gay pornography. I got back in bed with a thermos of green tea, a huge box of tissue and a big paper bag to toss my germs in. The phone rang. It was Sweat Shirt calling to see how I was. I told him how bad I felt that he accepted my cancellation so easily the day before. I told him the door bell was ringing, but I was too sick to answer.

"Go, see who it is," he said.

"I don't want to," I said while peering through the shutter slats to see who it was. The doorbell kept ringing. The dog kept barking.

"Go see who it is," he insisted.

I struggled with my bathrobe and the phone at my ear as I made my way to the front door and looked through the peep hole.

"Oh, my God," I shrieked into the phone. "It's you and I look awful."

I opened the door so he could enter with a bag of takeout deli chicken noodle soup, flowers and cough syrup. But all I could think about was how awful I must look and smell in sweaty flannel pajamas, no makeup and hair every which way. I begged him to take off his thick glasses, but he insisted it didn't matter. Nevertheless, I darted to the shower with greater speed than I had shown in the past two days. I clocked myself at 3.7 and emerged if not looking better, smelling sweeter. I put on a green chenille robe that matched my complexion. I was still too sick for Victoria's secrets. I felt more like the picture of Dorian Gray.

There would be no kissing, minimum hugging, but foot rubbing was quite comforting if it stopped at the knee. I took two teaspoons of his purple cough syrup, sipped the hot chicken noodle soup and expressed my great appreciation for his friendship, devotion, and computer expertise. I promised, seductively, to repay his kindness if I ever recovered from this flu.

The phone rang. It was Sidney telling me my mail box was accepting his jokes again. I whispered that I had a gentleman caller over. He was shocked and impressed that I would let anyone see me in my sick state. He told me about the great show I had missed and asked if I needed him to shop for me. I told him my son would be over the next day to help.

My son did arrive fifteen minutes before the Super Bowl playoffs which he wanted to see on my new 40-inch Samsung with DVR and HD. He dumped the trash and emptied the dish washer when it had two more cycles to go. He finished the left-over pizza, chicken soup and assorted juices.

He did bring me a cup of tea during half time and expressed his shock at seeing me sick. He wondered if this was the beginning of my deterioration into old age. He assured me he would be around to take care of me, but would check after the next quarter to see what benefits I was entitled to in my long-term health policy.

The phone rang. It was Sidney telling me my mail box was full again and he didn't want me to miss his latest joke. I went to the computer and found a sweet message from Thursday Sweat Shirt eagerly awaiting our next visit, and telling me what a turn on that green chenille robe had been. The phone rang again, with Saturday Suit inquiring about my health.

"I'm still coughing and have no energy or appetite."

"That's good" his voice came through amplified. "You sound much better."

I knew he wasn't wearing his hearing aid. I coughed back, "I'm just reading old New Yorkers and trying to train Molly, my puppy, to bring in the paper and make chicken soup.

I turned my phone to mute, slid under the blankets and comforters and had a new appreciation for my solitude, independence, and status as a free-lance woman in sickness and in health, for better or for worse.

A Romantic Weekend

E. J. invited me to go with him to the Bay Area for his son's wedding. It would be our first weekend away together and I wasn't sure how I felt about sharing a bed with him. I didn't expect two rooms, but I did request two beds telling him I was a very restless sleeper. Trying to sound rather virginal with a blush in my voice, I explained that this would be a first...with him.

I knew we would be busy most of the time with the wedding events, but I figured there would be a little extra time for cable cars and romance. I gave a lot of thought to packing casual and more formal clothes, walking shoes and very sexy sandals for the wedding, a sweet little short white nightie with embroidered roses bordering the modest neckline. At E.J.'s advanced age, I didn't want to overwhelm him with the red, black and lacy gown I kept in my bottom dresser drawer, which had been converted to a late in life still-hopeful-chest.

The day before our departure, E.J. called to confirm plans and add a bit of information he had forgotten to mention on the previous fifteen conversations and E-mails we had exchanged about this weekend together. First, he told me we were not going to San Francisco, where I would have left my heart, but to Oakland where I would meet his children for the first time and see him in pajamas.

The second surprise was that we would not be traveling alone. Doris, his ex-wife and Selma, his 92-year-old sister would be joining us. He felt responsible for their care and was sure that I would understand. He advised that I pack light as he was sure his ex-wife and sister would need to bring extra bags for all their medications.

Departure Day arrived. The chaperones waited in the car while E.J. came to the door to get me and my one small case. His sister, Selma, was already seated in the front seat and it would have taken too much time and effort to transfer her to the back seat, where Doris was pushing and shoving her bags so I could find a place to sit. "It's a good thing you're so tiny" she said after greeting me with "I'm Doris, but everyone calls me Dee."

"I'm Nurse Nancy, but everyone calls me flight attendant," I felt like answering, but didn't. I smiled and reached over the bags and cane and walker and umbrella and shook her hand. Selma had a problem turning around in the front seat. She just waved a hand that was veined, manicured and encrusted in jewelry.

E.J. pulled his Lexus in front of the Burbank terminal and the two of us began to unload Selma and Doris, their bags, canes, jackets, scarves and walker. My assignment was to stay with them while he parked the car. It was a good thing that we got to the airport almost two hours earlier than suggested. It took almost thirty minutes to get Selma installed in a wheelchair and Doris back from the ladies room. We finally got to the gate and waited for them to call the people who needed help boarding. Doris and Selma were hoisted from the tarmac to the entrance of the plane. I took a picture of them waving to us.

The flight attendants were very confused about Mr. Jacobs sitting between two women with different names, while Mrs. Jacobs sat across the aisle. E.J. comported himself like a sheik with his senior harem, patting my knee possessively while first wife sitting across the aisle chatted incessantly, telling me more about E.J. than I wanted to know.

It was a short flight and a long disembarkation from the Oakland Airport. We had to get two wheelchairs to put the ladies into when they were lowered from the plane. After getting the luggage off the carousel and onto carts with me trailing behind carrying an assortment of jackets, umbrellas and miscellaneous bags, we trudged outside to get a taxi to take us to the hotel. By the time we arrived and checked in, I needed a stiff drink and a hot bath.

The second day, Doris and Selma, who were roommates, had stopped talking to each other and instead were using me to vent their exasperation with each other. Selma said over cocktails that evening, "Doris doesn't shut up. She even talks in her sleep between snores. I can't get a minute of rest."

Doris told me as we waited in the lobby for a taxi, "Selma complains about everything. The room's too hot. The room's too cold. The meat's too salty. She's probably complaining about me. And that E.J. is getting to be an old grouch, too. It must run in their family."

The wedding was Saturday night. I put on the light summer dress that I would freeze in later and the little sexy shoes that suddenly didn't fit in the hotel the way they had at Macy's. For some mysterious reason, my feet had swelled a size and the shoes pinched miserably. I rushed to the gift shop for a pair of expensive panty hose which didn't ease the pain. I began to wonder if all women close to E.J. developed walking problems.

E.J. now had to help Selma, Doris, and me to the taxi. During the ceremony and dinner at the restaurant, I slipped the sandals off for some relief. Blisters had already begun to form. I had been looking forward to dancing with E.J., but I had to disappoint him and watch him go off to dance with one of the bridesmaids. I sat between Doris and Selma who complained about the loud music and each other and wanted to leave early.

All three of us limped to the cab. E.J. wasn't doing that well either after his exertion on the dance floor. When we got back to our room, he was worn out from helping all three of us in and out of the cab and up the elevator. He was too exhausted for love making, and all I wanted rubbed were my feet.

The next morning I was back into comfortable Easy Spirits but limping a bit as I helped us get through the lines at the airport and back to Burbank. I pushed Selma's wheelchair in the terminal. Doris was leaning on E.J.'s arm and walking ahead of us. I couldn't help but observe what a nice couple E.J. and his ex-wife, Doris, made walking together. They were the same age, had three children, the same name and he was still supporting her in every way.

That was two years ago. The shoes went to Good Will. E.J. and I are still going to the movies every Saturday, and Doris and Selma had separate rooms at the last family Bar Mitzvah.

Global Warming

Joe and I used to work in the same school and would flirt occasionally at the coffee maker or the copy machine. He was happily married then and I was happily divorced.

We hadn't seen each other for five years when he called to tell me he had separated from his third wife and wanted to ask me out on a date. After the dinner and movie, we returned to my house for a glass of wine and to catch up on what we'd been doing the past five years. Joe filled me in on his ensuing divorce, making it sound agreeable, civilized and not the least bit bitter. Then he asked what I had been doing with my time since retirement.

"I've been writing," I told him.

"Are you doing your sexy memoirs?" he winked and grinned.

"Not exactly." I hated to confess. "What I have been passionately involved in this past year is a series of lessons on global warming."

He poured another glass of wine and tried not to look disappointed as I proceeded to tell him more than he wanted to know about the curriculum I had spent months creating. I brought out a box filled with examples of my work. I started with a letter from Mrs. Polar Bear begging the children of the world to save the melting glaciers and her twin cubs. While Joe struggled to suppress a yawn, I demonstrated the history of fossil fuel by pressing strips of colored felt on a black flannel board to represent millions of years of pressure that eventually produced a purple cut-out oil well, a black smudge of coal, a white dot of gas and a yellow light-bulb shape.

I performed all the parts of the Arctic Food Web paper bag puppet play, "Red Krill, Red Krill, What Do You See?" I even extracted the "Go Green" bingo game and asked if he wanted to play. I had to repeat my question because Joe nodded off for a moment. He awoke with a start and complimented me on the good work I had done.

"Do you want a cup of hot chocolate?" I asked, because he had his jacket over his chest like a blanket and was blowing on his hands. It was a cold November night and my house felt like Minnesota in an ice storm.

"I know I should put on the heat," I apologized, "but since this project I have become really aware of the importance of conserving fossil fuel."

Joe looked at his watch, which was hard to read because of the dim 60-watt fluorescent bulbs I had replaced in my lamps. Then he looked out the window at a light rain that was beginning to fall.

"Do you still live in Azusa?" I asked.

He nodded yes. His eyes that had once hinted of carnal delights now seemed to droop with drowsiness.

"How long a drive is it?" I wanted to know.

"About an hour" he said, yawning again. "Crazy thing is that I have to be in Hollywood tomorrow morning, just ten minutes from here."

I lifted my curriculum from my lap and placed all my other elementary school regalia on the table. He laid his request beside it. "Would you mind if I sleep over?"

"Here on the couch?" I asked, taking off my glasses.

He pressed the cushions as if testing a new mattress.

"Sure," he answered.

I thought about it. I looked out the window at the rain coming down. I considered turning the heat on. I said, "Well, I guess you can. I don't see any reason..."

Before I could finish, he jumped up, raced to his car and returned, carrying an umbrella, overnight bag, and toiletry kit. I walked to the linen closet for some sheets. I was even considering a reset of the thermostat when Joe began to help me with the bedding. His chin resting on a pillow, he looked down at me from his 6-foot height and sounding more like a sharp lawyer in a courtroom than Casanova in the boudoir, he asked me to reconsider his final resting place for the night.

"Should it be the living room sofa?" he began, "where sheets, pillow cases, and blanket would need to be laundered resulting in additional gas for the dryer and to heat the water, plus all that water needed to fill the machines and the coal required to generate the electricity? Then, of course, the extra lighting that would be turned on in two rooms, not to mention turning on the heat to keep the Chihuahua from freezing to death."

I looked at him in disbelief.

He smiled, "Your king-sized bed has enough room for two, wouldn't require additional bedding, extra lighting or more heat."

He had been listening, I smiled to myself. I did a quick recall of research estimating that the average American adult emits about 20 tons of CO_2 a year. Just turning on a light three hours a day generates 340 grams of carbon dioxide. No one ever did a study comparing the differing effects of the eco system on singles and couples. A lot has been said and written about egos, but what about ecos? I pondered our carbon footprints. Joe had very large feet and probably could generate a lot of thermal power in bed.

We were old friends. We'd known each other since the '70s. The night was unseasonably rainy and cold, probably due to climate changes.

"I haven't slept beside a woman in over a year," he confessed.

I silently calculated; it had been nearly a year since I'd spent the whole night with a man.

After a second of serious consideration, I relieved him of the bedding and placed it back in the linen closet. I took out an extra towel and handed it to him, pointing to the bathroom and down the hall to the bedroom. I turned down the thermostat, put a sweater on Chorizo the Chihuahua, and lit some candles that gave off a scent of romance.

Elder Hostile

It's just wonderful how y'all are keeping up with the rest of us. I hope I have your energy and vitality when I am your age. You are my role model."

This is what Estelle told me after a lunch in a very quaint paladar in Trinidad, on a recent college alumni tour of Cuba. She placed a piece of fish on my plate and I was sure she was about to cut it for me. I was prepared to knife her if she did.

Estelle had just bought 10 straw hats for her mah jong friends in San Antonio. Her husband, Bud, who always dressed in UCLA shirts, hats and probably underwear, was obediently carrying them for her. She was having trouble keeping up with me on the cobblestone streets and winding staircases, but I could never keep up with her in the market place.

Estelle's awe-filled compliments came after sexy CPA Laurie told me over a breakfast omelet that I reminded her of a math teacher she had in junior high who had the same spirit and hair style.

And Jeffrey's amazement at my similarity to his 90-year-old aunt, Sylvia Riskin, in Connecticut, left me ready to defect from the tour. He did say he knew I was younger, but his aunt loved to dance, and he could see me about to leap onto the stage of the Tropicana the night before, ready to shimmy and shake and do a Carmen Miranda imitation. I knew I shouldn't have had that third Cuba Libre or free cigar I picked up.

I was grateful that Oscar, the driver, helped me maneuver the high step from the bus down to the street. Assistance carrying my suitcase up a steep flight of stairs was also appreciated. But I didn't need Estelle or Laurie holding my arm as we crossed a busy Havana street, and Jeffrey could only take my hand if we were going to salsa in a local club. Anyone who calls me "young lady," unless it is someone older, gets hit over the head with my very large and heavy handbag. There were two or three other travelers from the alumni group who graduated before I did, and they were still driving at night and walking without canes.

I felt depressed staring at the fish on my plate that I had no trouble cutting with a fork. There were flies on the ceviche, and I wondered about the oil floating on the hot yellow soup. Then the musicians appeared on the sunny patio. Four older, dark-skinned men carrying drum, guitar, saxophone, guiro and other assorted Cuban folk instruments. My spirits lifted.

They started to play Cuban love songs with the same sexy spirit of the Buena Vista Social Club. I was the only one listening and applauding after each number. When lunch was over, I was the first to run up to them and buy a CD. I told them how much I loved their music. The leader patted his nappy white hair and said, "I play the old songs."

"They're the best kind," I said, as he autographed my CD and I pointed to my gray hair.

I had once vowed that I would never take a trip to an exotic tropical island in the company of another woman, especially a retired teacher. But here I was and whenever the music started and no one asked me to dance, I wished I'd chosen Milwaukee or Minneapolis as my vacation destination.

To overcome my depression in the shabby hotel in Sancti Spiritu, I placed a worn-out towel on the stained, once-elegant bedspread and put my legs up on the wall. My yoga teacher prescribed this as the best remedy for insomnia, depression and aging.

After 10 minutes of serious breathing and the mantra, "I breathe in to calm myself. I breathe out and smile," I resolved to be more tolerant of young people. After all, I had been one myself a long time ago.

Then I climbed into the old tub and turned on the shower that only managed a slight dribble from its rusty plumbing. I dried myself with the worn-out, grayish towel, and dressed in a slightly wrinkled skirt and a blouse I planned on dumping at the end of the trip, along with the sandals that were comfortable before my ankles swelled.

I made my way down the dark rickety staircase to the shabby lobby and out the door to the narrow porch facing the plaza. Estelle, Bud, Laurie, and several other fellow travelers were crowded around one of the round tables enjoying their *cerveza* and *mojitos*. They beckoned me to come and join them. Jeffrey ran to pull over a chair for me. It was a warm evening, or someone would surely have offered me a shawl.

"How are you doing, pretty lady?" Estelle drawled. "I love what you're wearing."

"Same thing I wore last night," I drawled back.

"Did you get some rest?" Laurie asked with concern.

"I'm rested and ready for a big *noche* in the *pueblo.*"

"Can I get you a *limonada* or a sherry?" Jeffrey asked.

"I'm really in the mood for something stronger," I said, looking towards the bar.

Before I could say Jack Daniels to Jeffrey, the woman serving drinks presented me with a *mojito*, winked mischievously and pointed to a gentleman sitting at the next table.

I turned around and to my surprise and the amazement of all the young folk at the table, the white-haired musician who had signed my CD that afternoon tipped his Cuban hat and smiled. I smiled back.

I took a sip of the sweet green drink and was grateful I can still cut my own fish, dance over cobblestoned streets, and appreciate the attention of a sexy man, whatever his age or mine.

The Renovator

I had great plans for the house when we bought it. I was going to modernize it, but we didn't have the money and my husband was not handy. The first thing I did myself was take down the original picket fence in front because it needed painting, the clinging roses needed food and trimming, and the gate was falling off the hinges.

I had hoped to square all the arches and lay black and white linoleum over the hardwood floors. I removed the carpeting as a start, and my mother later thought that was the cause of my divorce. If only we had wall to wall carpeting everything would have been okay.

If only my husband had finished painting the nursery before the baby was born. If only he had finished steaming the wallpaper off in the hall, which I called the Great Chinese Wall because it was taking almost as long to finish as the one in Asia. My husband only painted it during the half-times of basketball and football games and the summer seventh-inning stretches of baseball games.

He was shocked when I asked for a divorce. No one else was. He said he had me on a pedestal and couldn't understand why I was so bothered just because the hall wall was taking three years to finish and door knobs were falling off the doors and one entire room was filled with his old newspapers and stock-market charts. I told him the pedestal was chipped, needed paint, and weeds were growing out of the cracks.

The very day he finally moved out, I met Ricardo Caraballo on the tennis court where I was playing with my women friends. Just the way he put the tennis ball in my hand and put top spin on his serve I could tell he wanted me for more than a doubles partner. I wasn't ready or interested that day, but I was a few Saturdays later when I agreed to a lunch at a nearby Mexican restaurant.

Over several Margaritas and a few refills of chips and salsa, Ricardo told me he had been a pilot, had a small airline, and flew Richard Burton and Liz Taylor to Puerta Vallarta. He told me he had been a conscientious objector during World War II and was shot down in Africa where a German prisoner doctor saved his leg from amputation. He told me stories about growing up on a ranch next to Will Rogers' polo field. He told me his father built Marion Davies' swimming pool near the beach. He told me how he used to fly contraband shrimp from Baja to Burbank, until he had to abandon his plane in San Felipe, Mexico.

They were all wonderful stories, but nothing impressed me as much as learning he was a pool builder, had been a contractor and knew everything about plastering, wall papering, painting, plumbing, electricity, tile, bricklaying, and home construction.

I invited him over for sangria and brisket.

When I told him I was a teacher in Pacoima, I saw romance ignite in his dark and beautiful eyes. He found me, a valley school teacher, more attractive than his first ex-wife who had been a beauty queen, his second ex-wife, a ski champion, and even the famous Liz Burton who had been a passenger on the small airline he had owned.

The next time he came over, he brought his tools and started with the door knobs, working his way to the leaky faucets and the toilet, and eventually into my bedroom and *mi corazon*.

This was the man who picked me up at school on his Harley Davidson, called me *Chispa* and taught me naughty Spanish words which I used inappropriately with the PTA president. He was the same man who shocked everyone at the faculty party by diving into the principal's pool nude. This was the man who taught me how to improve my skills on the tennis court and in the bedroom. He could pierce ears, give a bikini wax, barbecue a turkey, install a new toilet, and birth a foal.

His greatest gift to me was taking old bricks from the yard and covering an ugly cement fireplace in the den. He would even have built a pool and spa if the ex-husband had been a little more generous with child support. Ricardo Caraballo became a hero to my two preadolescent boys. He would put our bikes on top of his station wagon and drive to the beach where we could ride, or to Ojai where he could show off how good he was on a horse, or fly us to San Diego, or sail us to Catalina.

I reconnected him with his Mexican roots. When I met him, he said he was of Basque descent. After a few months, he was a born-again Mexican bringing me his

homemade enchiladas. I dragged him downtown to the
Million Dollar Theatre for Mexican movies and the
Mercado on Broadway for tacos.

I schlepped him to Zacatecas on a bus so he could
be with me when I studied Spanish at the *Instituto* and
to Yucatan ruins which I thought would be our
honeymoon but wasn't. I changed him for a while from
being a scotch and sirloin dude to a salmon and quiche
guy. He told me at the beginning of our romance that he
loved Ingmar Bergman's films about suffering Swedish
women. At the end, he changed back to John Wayne
westerns, took his tools and toys and rode off into the
sunset on his Harley Davison with another woman
clinging to his T-shirt.

Ricardo Caraballo was a brilliant story teller, a
wonderful dancer, a skilled draftsman, and a Don Juan
with a beautiful smile and a limp few people noticed.
He was single when I met him, but somewhere along
the line another woman came into his life and I didn't
find out until I received terrible drunken calls from her
in the middle of the night. I should never have trusted a
man who carried a change of clothes in his car. He used
to warn me that, "It's a jungle out there on Ventura
Boulevard."

He was very much a predator with a soft, sweet
voice and a warming touch. But looking back, I didn't
end up the loser. He gave me a new confidence in
myself as a woman and as a tennis player. He extended
my Spanish vocabulary, improved my pronunciation
and built a beautiful brick fireplace in my den.

My sons were the envy of their junior high friends,
who wished their mother had a boyfriend who owned a

motorcycle, rode a horse, could fly an airplane, sail a boat, and fit four bikes on top of his station wagon. After many years, he is now remembered with fondness as the great renovator.

All the Luck

Jan and I were having lunch at a cute little Mexican restaurant in Ventura. We talked about our grown-up kids and their problems, our old dogs and their vet bills, plays, musicals, and, of course, men. We always got around to men. We could be hiking in the Sierras or at a serious lecture, or sunning ourselves on the beach when we inevitably got around to men, the good and bad men in our lives and our hopes for the future ten or twenty years we expected to live.

It was the first time Jan mentioned her fall.

"I was on the way to the movies with my granddaughter when I tripped over nothing, no reason at all, and almost fell into the arms of this man crossing the street in a motorized wheelchair. He had the most beautiful smile and the sexiest brown eyes. I felt like such a klutz."

Jan was the kind of woman who would see beyond a person's limitations, physical or mental, and into their souls. She was also an actress, singer, and voice teacher, and thrived on drama. She had sung in Las Vegas, but not topless, she was always quick to add. I didn't know her when she was the young ingénue in musicals in high school and college, or the star of local, small theatre productions.

She was still beautiful in her mid-sixties, tall and statuesque with hazel eyes and light brown hair and very good bone structure. I could imagine her in high school as the girl all of us less popular, less talented, shorter, fatter, and darker-haired girls wanted to be like.

She had been a cheer leader, the lead in the senior musical, a good swimmer and volleyball player, and dated the star of the basketball team whom she married a few years after graduation. She was also the girl who was especially kind to those less popular kids who trailed after her in the school halls, or wanted to sit next to her in the cafeteria, or might have been in a wheelchair, or even worse, the boys who brought water to the players waiting on the bench during basketball and football games.

Her beauty was more subtle now; her voice was much weaker in the last few months. Now this problem of falling and complaining of joint pain was troubling. Still, the mischievous smile as she talked about the attractive man in the wheelchair proved that the same high school girl passion for rescue and romance had not waned.

Jan had been divorced from her high school basketball-star husband for several years, but there were two men in her life that we could talk about. One was a retired actor and director. He had been her passionate, jealous lover when they first met, but now after several years they were just platonic friends. They went to dinners and took little trips, but slept in separate beds.

It's better this way," Jan said. "We get along much better as friends."

"And what about your new man?" I asked.

"You mean- Bert?" she laughed. "I've actually known him since third grade. We went all through school together. I hadn't seen him for years, and then we met a few months ago at a friend's funeral. He's asked me out a few times."

"Is he a theatre person?" I asked.

"Not really," she answered. "He was the audio visual monitor in high school; the one who set up the projector or helped back stage. Now, he's more a country western cowboy kind of guy. He wears Navajo belt buckles and cowboy boots, and loves to go to swap meets and garage sales."

Neither of the two men in her life was with her when she got the news about the cause of the fall near the movies and the one on her stairs and the other one at work. It wasn't caused by the pinched nerve one doctor suggested or a reaction to steroids as another diagnosed.

It wasn't MS or Parkinson's, as I feared. It was worse. Jan finally responded to the many messages I had left on her answering machine. I knew immediately by the sound of my friend's voice that it was not good. She wept, "They think I have ALS, Lou Gehrig's disease."

Jan's three daughters rallied to her support. Her gentlemen friends were there for her. Philip, the aging Shakespearean actor, one-time lover and now friend, finally was able to tell her how much she meant to him. Bert was there to look after her little dog, Kiddo, and also to help her move from the split-level town house to a rented house without stairs. He had wanted to take her on a camping trip before she got the bad news, but Jan had in a very kind way explained that maybe it was better for their relationship if they kept it platonic. With some relief, Bert responded, "Ya betcha."

Several months passed. It wasn't easy to reach Jan. She was busy seeing doctors, nutritionists, and therapists in different cities and participating in a variety of experimental healing programs. I finally was able to get past the answering machine and hear her voice. It sounded shaky, but her spirits were high. There was so much she wanted to share. We set a date for lunch.

This time we went to a restaurant close by. I drove and let her out by the door so she wouldn't have far to walk while I parked. She leaned on my arm as I helped her to a seat.

"Well," I said, "so what's new?"

I expected to get a full report on her ALS treatment, but instead she looked at me and said, "I'm in love. I have a sweetheart."

"Is it Phil, or Bert, or the man in the wheelchair with the beautiful eyes?"

"None of the above," she said. "It's Doug, another friend from high school. I met him at a high school reunion."

I was sorry it wasn't Audiovisual Bert who had had an unrequited, unreciprocated crush on her for all these years. I thought maybe Shakespearean Phil finally woke up and proposed.

"I'm sorry, too," she confessed. Bert had been so steady and loyal. And Phil was trying to make amends. But it was Doug who finally captured her heart and imagination and made her laugh and blush like a teenager.

The three men remembered Jan as she had been in high school and as a glamorous actress. They seemed blinded to the reality that she was having trouble walking and her speech was slurred. To them her eyes still sparkled, and her dimple showed when she smiled. She still stirred their ardor as if they were young again.

Two months later I received an invitation to her wedding and thought, "This kind of thing only happens in the movies."

Doug with the gray hair and a wonderful sense of romance and humor was the one who proposed to the girl he had a crush on since high school. She was honest about her prognosis. She was in a wheelchair. He knew what the future held for both of them. But they were determined to enjoy each moment.

I went to the wedding held at her daughter's home. Her doctor spoke before the ceremony about the importance of trusting your heart. An actor friend conducted the ceremony with grace and tenderness. Jan was held up by her brother and Doug. It was as if little hearts hovered over them. They smiled and kissed when they were pronounced man and wife. We were outdoors. There was a gentle breeze in the late afternoon. Tissues and hankies were clutched and dabbed and tucked in pockets and purses as we all posed for photos. A recording of her voice singing "Funny Valentine" played in the background.

I visited Jan a few weeks later. She could no longer speak. She communicated with a key pad that transmitted her words in another voice. She had difficulty swallowing. Doug was at her bedside making sure she was comfortable.

I related Jan's condition to another friend and expected her to sigh sympathetically, but instead she said, "Imagine that! Jan, with ALS and a dim future, had three men wanting to marry her. What are we doing wrong?"

I think Jan would appreciate that. No one wants to feel they are a victim. It's not a role she ever wanted to play.

Zircon Lil

L ast month was my birthday. My Saturday suitor, E.J., presented me with a very small token of his affection which he attributed to his losses in the stock market and the world financial crisis. He asked if I wanted to exchange it, as I had before with an expensive cashmere sweater he had given me before the recession. I changed that one sweater from Nordstrom's for a coat, 2 blouses and a bracelet from Macy's. The next Christmas he gave me a Scrabble set from Walgreens Drug Store.

"No, I'll keep the necklace," I said, and he quickly removed the price tag and put it in his pocket making it impossible to return his gift.

Saturday Suit is a kind and generous elderly gentleman whose birthday card from the Alzheimer's Foundation was not very romantic and whose gifts are not nearly as valuable as those he tells me he gave his late wife.

One of my late gentlemen friends who happens to be resting at the same cemetery as Saturday's wife, was not as distinguished, successful, educated or rich as Saturday, but he was very generous.

Dan was the sweetest, kindest, dearest and most giving person I've ever known. For the years we went together, I felt richer, taller, younger, thinner, prettier and sexier than I really was. He made me feel like a queen which made it hard for him to measure up to my royal expectations no matter how hard he tried.

Dan was a slender man with prematurely white hair and a ruddy, Humphrey Bogart face. He was a lively mixture of genes inherited from an Irish Catholic alcoholic mother and a New York Jewish tap-dancer father. Dan was recruited for a short time on a minor league baseball team and never finished high school. He was street smart and tough. When I met him, he ran a rehabilitation workshop for mentally disordered sex offenders. They shrink-wrapped educational materials for a local printer. The first gift he gave me was a box of multiplication bulletin boards to share with teachers at my school. I became very popular as a distributor of hot times-table charts.

The second gift was given to me on our first Christmas together. He surprised me with a pair of crescent-shaped sparkling earrings.

"Do you like them?" he asked.

"I love them," I answered, kissing him appreciatively. "I've never had such elegant jewelry."

"Now, take care of these," he warned, knowing how careless I could be with earrings and bracelets.

Just the way he said that made me realize the value of his gift. I put the velvet box in a special corner of my scarf drawer, hidden under a thick bandana. Dan asked on every date why I wasn't wearing them.

"They're for special occasions," I told him. "I only wear them when I get dressed up or for weddings, anniversaries, or New Year's Eve."

Every time I did wear them, someone would compliment me and Dan would beam.

I didn't wear the earrings all the time because I was afraid I would lose them or break them and Dan would be so upset. Even though he was the kindest, dearest, sweetest, most generous man who has ever loved me, our relationship was beginning to fray at the edges.

Dan's bad grammar and mismatched use of pronouns and verbs like *you wasn't wearing my earrings*, was beginning to irritate me like fingernails on a chalk board. And there were those missing front teeth which he refused to see a dentist about. And there was too much drinking and smoking. And most of all because I met another man.

I hated to give up the cigarettes and our Sunday tennis doubles and the Frank Sinatra records and paella pan he lent me and the new solar-system bulletin boards, but the time had come to say goodbye. I did not give back the earrings. But I did promise myself to never wear them while with another man. I would only wear them to family gatherings and school events. I have my ethics.

The years passed and I still wouldn't wear Dan's earrings no matter how fancy the affair. When I did take them out for my brother's 50th anniversary party, I noticed that two of the precious stones were missing. I went to the neighborhood jeweler and told him that I wanted to replace the missing diamonds.

"How much will it cost?" I asked.

He put the jeweler's loupe to his eye. He looked at the earring. Then he looked at me, waiting expectantly. He looked at the earring again and then at me with a slight nod of his head that made me ask, "You mean they're not diamonds?"

He shook his head and told me they were very nice earrings, but the stones were zircons. They would be a lot cheaper to replace.

Dan may have been laughing from some heavenly tennis court. The jeweler couldn't suppress a chuckle behind the counter, but the truth of it is that I had the last laugh. Now I could pull out that little velvet box and wear those sparkly earrings whenever and with whomever, and I was free of guilt and several dollars richer by replacing less pricey zircons which may be a girl's second best friend.

Venus and Roger

J eri decided she didn't want them anymore. They were too small for her size-eight feet which swelled when she played hard tennis.

"Does anyone want these shoes?" she yelled. In a timid voice I answered from the bench, "Can I try them?"

"Sure."

Jeri tossed them at me in her grand tennis diva manner as if she had just made a generous donation to a shoeless person or the Valley Home for the Aged.

They were almost new New Balance court shoes, cloud white with a sky blue outline around the trademark N. I felt like Dorothy when she found the sparkling red slippers under the house. I was leaving dufferdom and the old senior-citizen bench, waiting to enter center court with the young, middle-aged semi-retireds.

"They fit," I lied, determined to grow into them by adding a pair of heavy-duty socks. I was honored to put my size 71/2 feet into Jeri's size-8 shoes, even though there was a lot of space between my toes and the leather. I was even happy that Jeri was talking to me and knew my name.

I was, after all, a new member of the Plaza tennis club located in a public park squeezed between the freeway and Sears.

It is not to be compared with the exclusive Los Angeles Tennis Club. Anyone with $15 can join our group. The club attracts a variety of tennis players ranging in age from twenty to eighty, and represents the diversity of Los Angeles.

There was Manny, the Ultimate Fighter, who, every time I played with him, began with, "We got to win" in his heavy Armenian accent. Teddy, from the Philippines, was quite handsome when he shaved and wore his false teeth. Whenever he placed the ball where no one could get it back, he'd laugh, "Nobody home."

There were women, too, who seemed to have rubbed on some male testosterone with their 15 UHF sunscreen; Wilma cursed like a hockey fan instead of a retired kindergarten teacher and Sally, who grunted like Sharapova, but looked like Barbara Bush.

The star of the courts was Jeri, who had long legs, a shapely figure, and youthful face even before the cosmetic surgery. She liked to win, big time. Being her partner was stressful, and playing against her could be humiliating.

She and her partner, Dick, ended their set. As winners, they challenged Herb and me to the next set. We were told to warm up. Herb was tall, thin and uncoordinated in body movement and clothing. He wore an African safari hat, pads on his knees, a brace on his arm, and sweatbands on his wrists. His dark brown socks kept slipping into green sneakers, meant for the deck of a sailboat, not a tennis court. There may have been a time many years ago when he was attractive and a good tennis player. Many, many years ago.

My partner and I were definitely no match for Jeri and Dick who wanted us to speed up so they could bagel us with a 6-love win and take on the stronger competition approaching the bench.

"Hurry up and warm up," Jeri ordered.

I was about to take off her shoes and put my old ones back on. I reached down to unlace them but couldn't. There was a soft light, like an aura emanating from them. I stood up and realized that they no longer felt too loose. They hugged my feet like soft gloves. I did a few calf stretches. I jumped up and down and felt light on my feet, as if there were hidden coils in the soles of the shoes. I sprang onto the court and faced Herb for the warmup. It was embarrassing. Herb lobbed everything over my head and into the next court. I couldn't practice any net returns.

We struggled for about five minutes while Jeri, Dick and some of the B-plus players on the bench chatted and laughed together. Then our opponents took their places. I was nervously springing up and down in Jeri's shoes.

"Herb," I said, sounding like Manny, the boxer, "We've got to win!"

He laughed, "I'm no Roger Federer, you know."

"Today you are," I snapped back. "Imagine his spirit invading your body."

"Well, you're no Jeri," he came back at me, pointing to our opponent.

"No," I said. "Today I'm Venus Williams in Jeri's tennis shoes."

They let us serve first. I was so nervous. I tossed the ball into the air and swung, completely missing it. I tried a second time and the ball went into the net. Double fault.

Then I took a few deep breaths and an easy hop and served the ball that came in low and hard. Jeri missed it completely. Herb, who was beginning to think he really was Roger, made some amazing shots at the net. We won the first game. The players waiting on the bench gave us the thumbs-up sign. Jeri wasn't laughing. She was at the base line ready to serve.

By some miracle, I was able to return her hard serve and even get those drop shots sliced at the net. I was jumping higher than usual and smashing Jeri's hard- driving backhand. I was at the baseline for a lob and then over to the other side of the court for a top-spin return that shocked Jeri, the guys on the bench, and even me.

My partner just waited at the net, lifted his hairy arm and smashed everything that came near him. I got what he couldn't reach. The score was 5-4. Herb was running out of Federer juice and let me poach and intercept. He didn't seem to care. He had never come this close to beating Jeri. We had been playing for over an hour without a break. I served. It was an ace.

Then Jeri made one of her hard, deep-down-the-middle shots. I returned it and Dick sliced it to the other side of the court. My New Balance friends, Lefty and Righty, carried me to the net so I could drop in the winning point.

The bench cheered us. Fists and thumbs up. High fives all around. Dick shook our hands, offered a sportsman-like compliment and thanked his partner Jeri, who without a word, zipped up her racket bag and marched off the court in her size-eight and one-half Nikes.

"Thanks for the shoes," I called after her, but she was already in her Lexus.

It wasn't a love game, but Herb did smile down at me and ask, "Would you like some of my Gatorade, Venus?" I took a sip and peered up at him from behind my dark glasses. By God, if there wasn't a slight resemblance to Federer. He could have been his father or grandfather.

I looked at my feet. The shoes were a little big, but I felt that with heavy socks I would grow into them. And as for my hat size, as I swaggered off the court, immeasurable!

Lost Verizon

There I was, sitting in front of my forty-inch TV at four in the afternoon watching Turner Classic Movies *Lost Horizon* for the tenth time. I listened to Ronald Colman's unforgettable voice and waited for my lover to call. My lover didn't sound like Ronald Coleman. He could do a better Cary Grant imitation, even though he was too young to really remember either one of those actors in their prime. I was always surprised that he remembered me in my prime, but then he had a school-boy crush on me when he was in his mid-thirties and I was in my early forties.

Over the years, he had seen me through a series of older gentlemen companions, and I had advised him on the young women in his life. After the death of several daddy men and his dissolved relationships, we sought comfort in each other's arms. We created our own Shangri-La in my garden condo. He matured without losing his boyish charm. I stayed the way I looked when he felt the first pangs of passion, twenty years before.

Liver spots vanished. Lines and wrinkles faded. Any puffiness on face or body flattened in Shangri-La, in the Mt. Everest Garden Complex on the corner of Himalaya and West Tibet.

Even after he moved out of the Valley where I lived to another city a few hours away, he would arrange to see me at least twice a month. Because we wanted our time spent alone and intimately, I would plan a candle-lit dinner, soft music and maybe a sexy Netflix selection. The dessert would always be left uneaten as we ended the evening on my red sateen sheets with moonlight filtering through the shutters and softening all age lines. The temperature was controlled by thermostats, fans, and our emotions.

He would call me on his mobile when he was thirty minutes away so I could apply the last strokes of blush and lip gloss and uncork the wine. This went on for several years with only the menu and my hair color changing. Then on our last evening together, he noticed me serving frozen left-overs from a dinner two weeks before, and I noticed him suppressing a yawn when I excitedly told him about a happening in my life. There was also a longer interval between meetings. That was when I decided we needed a change. I felt we needed to leave Shangri-La if even for one night.

"Oh, no, baby," he argued. "I love what we have here together."

"Are you tired of my cooking?" I asked.

"I love what you cook, but if you're tired of cooking, we could have Chinese or Tibetan delivered next time."

"No, no," I said. "I think the time has come for us to leave Shangri-La, maybe meet in Hollywood for dinner and a movie near your new digs."

"Really, honey, are you sure you want to leave the Valley where we've shared so many wonderful moments in your kitchen and bedroom? Think about the risk we're taking."

"The risk of someone seeing you with a woman so much older?" I asked. "You haven't gotten married, have you?"

"Of course not, Sweetheart," is the way he'd left it two weeks ago, and now I am waiting for my phone to ring, "Hey, Mrs. Robinson." There it goes. I put *Lost Horizon* on pause and went in search of my ringing Verizon. It was under a stack of AARP magazines.

"Hello, my Darling," I answered in my most seductive voice. "I'm ready to meet you anywhere out of the Valley."

"Are you sure?" he asked with doubt and fear in his voice.

"Yes," I answered. "It's a wonderful test of the strength of our relationship."

His voice then changed from sexy to GPS as he gave me directions on how to get to a restaurant in Hollywood. "Take Laurel Canyon south…"

I wrote everything down because I don't trust my memory any more. I applied a fresh coat of blush, gloss, and White Diamonds.

"Are you sure you want to go through with this?" he asked again, sounding like Margo's boyfriend in *Lost Horizon.*

"Yes. I'm tired of Shangri-La. I'm ready for Hollywood."

I hated to leave just as Margo and her boyfriend were beginning their trek out of Shangri-La – she, young and sexy at ninety; he, sixty years her junior and still madly in love with her.

"It's just a movie," I said to myself, setting the DVR to record before grabbing my car keys and phone and making my way to the garage. Traffic over Laurel Canyon to Sunset Boulevard was congested. I got stuck behind a sightseer and there was no way to pass with the steady stream of cars coming in the opposite direction. I didn't think I'd be able to meet my sweetie at five. Better call him.

OMG, where's the damn phone? I was sure I had transferred it to my handnbag along with the directions to where we were going to meet.

It might have slipped under the seat. We were moving slowly enough for me to try to reach it. I needed to get it to call and find out whether the restaurant was on Vine or Fountain or Gower. It had started to rain, making it hard to maneuver around the curving, slippery canyon road.

At the first red light, I managed to pull the lost Verizon from under my seat. I blindly pressed in his number. I started to leave a message, but was immediately disconnected. I was nearing Mulholland. I tried calling him back, but wasn't getting any response. There was no place to pull over and park. Then my phone rang, *Hey, Mrs. Robinson.* I opened it to talk.

"Hello," came out strangely.

"Hey, babe, is that you? I'm waiting for you on Sunset and..."

There was a bright light flashing behind coming from a black and white car with a driver signaling me to pull over. I put down my phone and parked in the first opening I found.

The police officer came to my window. He asked if I was aware of a law that said you couldn't use phones when driving. I looked over at the young fellow and struggled to find my voice, which suddenly crackled with age.

"No, Sonny. I didn't know about such a law. I'm having a problem keeping up with these modern times."

He asked to see my license. I pulled it out of my wallet and was shocked to see how I had changed. My hair was white.

"Well, Ma'am," he said politely, "seeing your age and remembering my own grandmother, I'm going to let you go this time. But I suggest you get a blue tooth, and maybe an Android, something a little more updated."

"Sure, Officer," I cackled as I made my way back down the hill hoping that Shangri-La had not been washed away forever.

Carlota's Gardener

Rosario is one of the kindest men I know. He is a good listener which is a rare quality in men these days. When I go out the back door to greet him or give him a check for his services, he turns off the edger or blower and comes over to me. He asks me how I am, as if he is really interested. I find myself confiding in him about my aches and pains and personal problems. His eyes express sympathy and concern if I am talking about my health, my work, my family or my relationships.

Rosario, under different life circumstances, should have been a therapist rather than a gardener. I knew a psychiatrist who probably would have been happier as a gardener, because unlike psychoanalysis, the fruits of a gardener's labor are instantly apparent.

Together, we stand admiring the freshly mowed lawn, and inhale the scent of the beautiful roses my best friend, Carlota, planted before her untimely death. The roses are in full bloom, blushing pink and flaming red. Rosario and I call them the Carlota Roses, Carlota's *nombre de pluma* in the many Spanish classes we took together.

It was Carlota who recommended Rosario when I was looking for a gardener. Our eyes moisten as

Rosario and I share remembrances of our beloved friend. I remember her green thumb. He remembers her tan legs. I remember her in garden gloves and a hat bending over to plant the roses. Rosario also remembers her bending over.

I even remember her mentioning that he had asked her out when he was between wives. The picture of Carlota, tall and elegant in a long tailored skirt, a flowing silk scarf and the high-heeled pumps she always wore, dancing with much shorter and younger Rosario in a sweat-stained T-shirt barely fitting over his ample belly and a straw sombrero seems very incongruous. I'm sure that Carlota prepared a lovely polite and tactful rejection that Rosario graciously accepted.

"Do you still see your *viejo?*" he asks me. "The old guy with the Lexus?" he adds.

"Oh yes," I laugh. "He's still kicking, but does have a problem walking."

I ask Rosario about his children and his second wife, the woman he imported from Zacatecas after his first wife left him. Sad-faced Lupita comes sometimes to help rake the leaves. After several years in this country, Rosario tells me she still hasn't accepted her new language and older husband.

Que lastima! I click my tongue sympathetically.

"It is also a shame," he says, "that your *viejo* doesn't take you dancing since you love it so much."

I tell him that I go myself to a Mexican Restaurant on Tuesday mornings to dance. They have a big band of retired musicians that play old favorites.

"It's good exercise," I say, doing a little two-step.

"En la mañana?" he asks, not sure he heard me correctly. "Wouldn't you like better to go at night with me sometime?" he asks.

I stop moving my body to Benny Goodman when I realize how intently Rosario is listening and looking at my face that is bare of makeup, mascara, blush, lipstick, or sunglasses.

I look back at him a little flushed by his invitation. I notice for the first time his trimmed little salt and pepper moustache, his white, even teeth, and the expression in his soulful dark eyes which has changed from empathy to desire.

"I had always this feeling for you," he pats his heart. "You are a very good woman."

"But what about your *esposa*, Lupita?" comes out of my mouth.

"A man needs passion in his life," he replies with a yearning catch in his voice.

He is about to reach out to me with his hand which has just edged my lawn, spread fertilizer, and pulled my weeds. I feel he is about to pull me to him. I step back against the screen and wrinkle my nose.

"Something is burning----in my kitchen," I lie.

I don't want to hurt Rosario's feelings. He has done so many extra favors for me, lifting, moving, disposing of dead rats, fixing sprinklers. I am not offended. I am really flattered, but I have to remind him that I am much older, we are not of the same religion, and he is married. Mrs. Chatterley didn't have this problem with her gamekeeper. After all, he wasn't married. She was.

With one hand on the door knob and the other on his extended hairy arm, I thank him for the invitation.

"Gracias. Maybe when my knee, back, elbow and shoulder heal, and my arthritis is better, I'll be more receptive," I tell him. "Something is surely burning inside my oven," I whisper, backing myself off the porch, but careful not to close the door completely.

Once inside the safety of my kitchen, I also tell myself to be careful to add the next time I wish for a younger man who is healthy, likes to dance, and is bilingual, that he should also bear a closer resemblance to Antonio Banderas, or Javier Bardem.

Harout and Masha

Mirishka, my manicurist and the Ukrainian icon of budget cuts, sent me to Avik knowing I needed hairstyling and he needed clients. I was the only one in his salon who didn't speak Russian and had gray hair.

"You want coffee, tea, water?" he asked before draping me with a protective cape and leading me to the sinks. I could tell that unrehearsed small talk didn't come easy. While he was blow-drying my hair and twirling the styling brush like a sculptor working with wet gray clay, I conversed with him, sheltering my English, slowing the pace, gesturing to my head, short here, long back there, bangs in front.

"I used to teach English to immigrant students," I told him as he finished with the spray can. "You just passed the hair test." I smiled and thanked him. I also thanked Mirishka who in the coming months achieved Sainthood.

On my return visit a month later, Avik asked me to teach him English.

"You're doing fine," I told him, "especially for someone who's been here only a year."

"No," he said. "I need be better. I want be professional."

Even though I had retired from the teaching profession and wasn't sure I wanted this commitment, his plea was sincere and I couldn't refuse. We agreed on a price and arranged for him to meet at my house when he finished work on Tuesdays. I greeted him at the door the first night, feeling like Bette Davis in *The Corn is Green* (but with a more hip hairdo). I realized during the first lesson that Avik is not the young poetic Welsh coal miner in the Bette Davis movie. After reading his composition about Lake Sevan in Armenia where there are "many hotels with good service and very good iskcan fish," I knew his gifts were hairstyling, not poetry. He does have the hands of a coal miner, though, which I expect is from the dyes he handles seven days a week. He even works on Sunday.

Avik has become special to me. He puts highlights into my hair and fattens me up with Armenian pastries. He has brought back into my life the joy and romance I felt for education when I was a young teacher in Pacoima. Avik is my last student and as precious as my first.

His name means good news in Armenian. He comes once a week to the classroom I set up on my dining room table. He carries his books and his homework in one hand and a Trader Joe's paper bag in the other. He has hairy arms and short cropped hair and very beautiful gray eyes. He is growing more handsome with each lesson.

After several "How are yous?" he hands the bag to me. It is filled with mangos, blueberries, dates and chocolate. I will have to explain to him that teachers get just an apple in the U.S. When we sit down, there is another *"How are you?"* and then he says, "You need haircut. I do you next time."

"Here?" I ask. "In my house?"

"Sure. No problem."

The next week he arrives with books and homework and a metal case filled with his hairstyling equipment. Instead of mangoes, he presents me with a new hair brush and a new hair style. Sometimes he compliments me and says, "Who did your hair? It looks fresh."

"Silly, you did my hair," I tease. He is pleased.

Then we do a lesson on future tense. Avik will cut my hair. Avik will blow dry my hair. I will pay Avik.

Next lesson, contractions and subjunctive: If you won't take my money for the haircut, I won't take your money for the lesson.

We fight. We argue. He wins. I can go to this shop on Sunday at eight in the morning or Thursday at nine in the evening. He will always "squeeze me in" which I needed to explain when I saw the puzzled look on his face. Next week, I'll work on idiomatic phrases like "That's cool, Dude."

For our first lessons, though, I asked him to tell me about himself. He told me he was born in Yerevan, Armenia. He was a flight attendant for Aeroflot. He recites, "Please fasten seat belt and what you want to drink?" He loves aviation. He loves his parents. He loves his country. He loves Los Angeles and he is beginning to love his new language.

His hope is to be "professional," which to him means owning his own shop or working in a salon in Beverly Hills. He feels that if his English improves, he will have a better chance of attaining his dream. I have entrusted him with my hair. He has entrusted me with his phonetic future. He thinks that vocabulary will pave his way to success. I think it's the hair color formula he uses and the clients he attracts. He writes every new word he learns in his notebook: lustrous, luxuriant, resolution, revolution, aspiration, perspiration, destiny, swell, and passion.

Avik's second homework assignment was to write a paragraph about the kind of woman he wants to marry. He wrote a sweet story describing a woman who is natural and kind and loves kids. He also told me about his birthday party where his cousins surprised him with a woman for the night. He blushed and apologized, but explained, "I need woman!"

So, I introduced him to Rebecca, a young woman about his age, also new to the city and monolingual English speaking. I planned a Thanksgiving dinner as part of my organic, holistic, sensory curriculum. Avik's assignment was to bring questions to ask her and a cake for dessert. He was very nervous about the meeting. I could tell by the way he started out with, "How are you?" three times. She answered, "Fine, but my ends are split and what do you suggest I do about my oily hair?"

I kept asking how he liked the cranberries, stuffing, and yams. Rachel kept asking about hair conditioners and scalp treatments. Avik brought a Russian wine and enough rich Armenian pastries for a party of ten. His final words to Rachel as they were leaving were, "Let me do your hair."

For Avik's birthday, I gave him a book of short stories by William Saroyan. We end each session reading aloud from his book. I had the pleasure of introducing a favorite California author whose family emigrated from Armenia. Avik was thrilled to pronounce for me the Armenian names and places Saroyan wrote about.

Avik is thirty-two. I'm old enough to be his--- teacher. At our last lesson, I had a chart of winter clothing. He named the mittens, scarf, parka and raincoat, but had a problem with the long nightgown.

"It's something women wear to sleep in," I explained.

"I don't like women wear nightgown," he confessed with a hint of embarrassment.

We are going to another level of learning in the curriculum I have designed. Next week, body parts.

I'll make some slight adjustments on the lessons I taught in the fifth grade, and I will be as professional as Bette Davis, but in a stylish hair style playing the teacher in *The Corn is Green*, eating Armenian pastries and mangos. That is, unless I rewrite this story as the Russian/Armenian version of *Harold and Maude*, *Harout and Masha*.

Last Tango in Hollywood

At 11:30 in the morning, my boss called to ask me for a favor. She told me she was supposed to have lunch with an old friend whose wife was dying of cancer.

"I just found out I have to be at a special meeting I can't get out of. It's too late to call him, and I don't want him to have to eat lunch alone. Will you meet him and send my apologies?"

"Sure," I answered, welcoming an excuse for a long lunch at Barragan's, my favorite Mexican Restaurant.

It was dark and cool inside. I told the hostess I was looking for a Sr. Lopez. She led me through a labyrinth of booths and bars past two other Senor Lopezes until we located Enrique Hank Lopez seated comfortably reading the morning paper. He had thick glasses, thinning hair, a prominent nose, a slouch when he stood up to greet me and the most elegant hand I had ever shaken. He had a voice that could convince juries and seduce women. He seemed pleased to meet me and have company for lunch. I was awed by his erudition and charm. He discussed his books about Katherine Ann Porter and his years at Harvard while I picked at my tostada and felt I was getting drunk on horchata and the way he was looking at me.

A month later I learned of his wife's death. I waited another month to send a note thanking him for the lunch and offering my condolences. Not too long after that, I received a phone call from him and immediately recognized his voice, deep and seriously sexy. He thanked me for the card and invited me to dinner. It was 1984, a great year for me. The Olympics returned to L.A. and so did Hank Lopez. I was a volunteer hostess at the Biltmore Hotel, and Hank was adjusting to a new law firm, the death of his wife, his fabulous apartment in West Hollywood and our budding romance.

I had been a Hank Lopez groupie since the first time I heard him address an auditorium full of school administrators. He commanded the attention of everyone with his words:

"I was delivered from my mother's womb by the village *curandera,* a gentle hunch-backed, dark-eyed midwife whose shiny black hair was evenly parted like the wings of a raven. *Este niño es puro indio,* she told my father. She herself was a full-blooded Tarahumara from the highlands of Chihuahuah."

Our romance took off like an Olympics event with exciting preliminaries in a variety of venues. Hank had a wide range of friends reflecting his eclectic career. There were the lawyer friends who teased him about being a born-again Mexican. He was supposedly the first Chicano to graduate from Harvard Law School.

He introduced me to politicos and judges who remembered when Hank ran for California Secretary of State in the 50s.

We met Hispanic writers, artists, and film producers who knew Hank as the author and journalist he became when he moved to Mexico after winning a large settlement as a personal injury attorney. Hank told everyone proudly that I was bilingual, which made me realize that love was deaf as well as blind.

Enrique Lopez was really the star. When he walked into a room filled with people he didn't know, he was sure they would like him, and they did, especially the women. He had been married three times and had three children he described with great paternal pride.

He was excited about leasing an apartment in an art deco building off Sunset and filling it with books and his collection of artifacts from Mexico. We were invited to parties and galas and fund raisers in hotels and parks and mansions. He loved to dance, especially the tango which he patiently taught me in the privacy of his apartment with little on but the music.

Hank gifted me with a beautiful silver bracelet from Taxco, a hand-woven serape from Guadalajara and silk lingerie from Trashy Underwear in West Hollywood.

I got him out of his Brooks Brothers suit to play tennis and take rigorous walks with my dogs. He recaptured a lusty enthusiasm for life and lovemaking.

Even though he assured me of his devotion and was serious about our relationship, I never completely trusted that he wouldn't be off with another *mujer*. Each time I tried to distance him, he'd entice me with an exciting invitation. I couldn't refuse a weekend in

Rosarita Beach at the house of a famous architect, a condo in La Jolla owned by a movie magnate from Mexico City, or a Carmel weekend we spent with Dan James, alias Danny Santiago, a black-listed Hollywood writer who wanted to thank Hank for defending his book, "Famous All Over Town."

Hank hadn't been feeling well. He dismissed his malaise as a touch of the flu, but still wanted to make the trip. He apologized that because of his poor health, it wouldn't be as romantic as he wanted it to be. I remember it as a sweet and tender time we shared together in a lovely guest house overlooking the Pacific.

When we returned to Los Angeles, Hank checked into the hospital before he was scheduled to give an important speech. He arranged for his son, Greg, and me to pick him up the night of the event from Cedars Sinai and escort him in a wheelchair to the hotel. He looked thin and pale as he stood behind the podium, but his voice was still deep and impressive.

"I am a mestizo," he began, "a genetic amalgam of Mexican Indian and diluted Spanish. From my father's side, I inherited a mesh of Aztec and Spanish genes. From my mother a mixture of Mayan, Olmec, and Sephardic Spanish."

When he finished his pitch for retaining one's culture and promoting bilingualism, he received a standing ovation as Greg and I wheeled him out of the ballroom.

"I'm always going to make an entrance in a wheelchair," he quipped. "So much easier than having to wait until the end of the program and sign autographs and shake hands."

He kissed me lightly as he got out of my car. He explained that Greg would stay with him that night. He wanted me to know that because of his failing health, our relationship would be changing. I understood and joked that I wouldn't force him to play tennis or tango for a while.

Hank died that night from congestive heart failure.

I helped plan his memorial. TV personalities, judges and long-time friends came to celebrate his life. I asked his brother to read the first page of Hank's autobiography. He skimmed what I handed him and thrust the pages back at me. "I can't read this," he said, "Hank wasn't delivered by a *curandera* in Chihuahua. He was born in a hospital in Denver."

Obituaries appeared in the *New York Times* which said Hank was 64. The *Los Angeles Times* said 65. I told the *Times* staff writer who contacted me for information that Hank spoke no English when he entered school. He ran home after his first day crying to his mother in Spanish, "they cut my tongue out."

His tongue grew back and he mastered the English and Spanish languages to become a brilliant lawyer, author, speaker, and the most interesting and accomplished man I ever had the pleasure to sleep with.

It's been thirty years since Hank's death. A few weeks ago, I went into a closet looking for a misplaced financial statement and in my search found a large leather brief case with gold letters, Enrique H. Lopez, stamped on one side. It was bulging with the type-written autobiography Hank had not finished, copies of magazine and newspaper articles he had written, reviews of his books, the guest book at his memorial, and two poems I had written about him.

In a note to Dan James after Hank's death, I wrote that I would never know another man like him. He was a charming blend of Harvard manners and barrio boyishness. My short time with him was filled with romance, poetry and some outrageously good times that changed my life profoundly.

Hank might not recognize me now with gray hair, wrinkles and a fuller figure. He'd have to get up very close and check me out with those long slender fingers of his. I always loved that his vision was poor.

It would be nice to sit across from him again eating sushi and drinking Corona beer or a margarita *sin sal.* Now that I'm older and retired, we'd have more quiet time to spend together. There is so much he wrote that I would want to talk about. I'd drive him *loco* with my questions.

"What was Lyndon Johnson's brother like?" I'd want to know.

"How did you do the research on those Uruguayan rugby players surviving by cannibalism?" I'd ask.

"How can I get copies of 'Eros and Ethos' and 'The Harvard Mystique'?"

Hank would probably smile, remove his glasses, and lean over and kiss me to make me shut up.

Crescent Heights
At your pad on Crescent Heights
we sipped tequila
on Friday nights.

Your tapered rosewood fingers
lifted bamboo skewers of yakatori.
We tangoed naked
on Saturday nights
on hardwood floors
above the city lights
reciting homemade verse
mixed with
mangos and jalapenos.

Final Ovation
Lopez
in lawyer blue
respectably grayed
thinner in the suit
that Brooks Brothers made,
got out of his hospital bed
to speak at a fund-raising dinner.
He strained
to lift his brief case
filled with medication
to ease his exhausted heart.
he did on that occasion
as always
play his seasoned voice
his instrument of grand persuasion
to a planned crescendo.
A final ovation.

Auld Lang Syne

Should auld acquaintance be forgot,
And never thought upon,
The flames of love extinguished,
And freely past and gone?
Is thy kind heart now grown so cold
In that loving breast of thine,
That thou canst never once reflect
On old-long-syne.

—Robert Burns

It was New Year's Eve. I sat alone in my kitchen feeling sorry for myself. I had no date or plans for celebrating the holiday. The last three significant men in my life had died and not at advanced ages or at the same time.

Dan died of lung cancer which was expected from a heavy smoker. Hank suffered a sudden onset of congenital heart failure which I feel I might have aggravated by pushing him to walk faster, play tennis, and engage in other equally strenuous love games. Mark informed me he had Parkinson's six weeks after we met, and I had already fallen madly in love with him by then.

After Hank's death, I made sure to check a new suitor's medicine cabinet the first opportunity I had, to analyze any drugs he might be taking for epilepsy, heart, diabetes, impotency, etc. My son strongly urged me to take a CPR class considering the age of men I was dating.

I sat at the kitchen table in my green chenille bathrobe, drinking a vodka and *7-Up* and replaying New Year's Eves of the past. I could remember the little black velvet sheath I wore with the earrings Dan gave me for Christmas. We were at the Holiday Inn letting the food cool as we danced every dance. Dan was the New York big spender who always smelled like Scotch and Marlborough's, and didn't mind hotels with average food and high prices as long as he was with me and could show off what a great dancer he was.

I blushed nostalgically at memories of New Year's Eve with Hank in his apartment off Sunset enjoying our last sexy tango in Hollywood and supping on sushi and Corona beer.

And then, about seven years after Hank's memorial, I was sipping Taittinger champagne and nibbling on caviar while Mark, the TV director, nibbled on me in front of a rustic condo fireplace.

I went through photos of my late lovers that had been tossed haphazardly in boxes. I was sorting them into three piles. There was Hank, smiling and looking distinguished in his horn-rimmed bifocals in Carmel; Dan, athletic, on the tennis court in Tahiti; Mark, looking dashing on the slopes in Lake Tahoe.

I drifted to the CD player where I listened to favorite old records that hadn't been converted to CDs yet. My hands were busy folding and stacking sweaters and lingerie neatly in drawers and arranging earrings in jewelry box compartments.

Oh dear, the first pair of earrings were the ones Dan gave me that I thought were diamonds until I went to replace a missing stone and found out they weren't and felt so relieved that I wouldn't feel guilty wearing them with other men.

When I started on the underwear drawer, I found the lingerie Hank gave me when we celebrated my birthday at Le Dome. The thought of Hank in his Brooks Brothers' suit and lawyerly demeanor shopping at that West Hollywood Trashy Lingerie store made me laugh and miss him even more. I held the little satin slip over my flannel pajamas sure that it would no longer fit or be admired, or be anything I could use if I ever took up quilting.

I closed the dresser drawer and collapsed on the sofa to listen to music when I realized my head was resting on the pillow embroidered with Dachshunds, one of the many silly dog gifts that Mark had given me with sweet whimsical cards written in his cramped Parkinson's handwriting. There were Doxie figurines, necklaces, pins, chopstick holders, one with wings and a halo, and three-piece ceramic dip dishes forming a wiener dog.

I put on a Stan Getz jazz record, one that I had borrowed from Mark's collection and never returned. It sounded like something he played on our first Christmas together in his condo. I was so impressed with his jazz and book collection.

I looked through my dusty collection of old records, many of which I had received as gifts. Dan was, of course, a Frank Sinatra man whose favorite song was *New York, New York.*

When Hank died, his kids told me to take anything I wanted. I took some of his Julio Iglesias LPs and an e.e cummings book of love poetry. He made me blush when he quoted lines like, "I love kissing the this and that of you."

I poured myself another drink before going to a dusty old keepsake box of love letters going back to college days. My God, I realized how immature and stupid I was to not have appreciated Paul, the teaching assistant who helped me write a term paper on T.S. Eliot, or the young man who sent me a single rose on opening night when I starred in *Hedda Gabler* and a card that said, "Man desires woman and woman desires the desire of man." It was signed Alexander Pope. It was a name I didn't recognize at that time because I hadn't taken that lit class yet.

I went to my desk which was a mess with remnants of Christmas wrapping and late cards I still hadn't opened. One peeked out from under a Macy's bill. I immediately recognized the handwriting. It was from a co-worker I hadn't seen since I retired. It was a funny card of a snowman with a melting heart, and a note saying, "I still have a crush on you. Let's do dinner in Chinatown next week. I'll call."

I threw all the old love letters back in their box. I dropped the nightie in the Goodwill bag. I turned off the record player.

It was almost nine. I decided not to watch the Times Square celebration in New York. Instead, I needed to go to bed early and dream of celebrating the

Chinese New Year with a sweet younger man — maybe in his late sixties.

Love Match

Bench on a public park tennis court. Morning.

IRV, a spry elderly gentleman of 85 dressed in tennis clothes and carrying a tennis bag and water bottle, enters. He wipes two bench seats with his towel before sitting down. He checks his watch, expectantly waiting for his partner to arrive. He watches the off-stage match as he waits.

RUTHIE, a shapely woman in her mid-seventies, dressed in several layers of tennis clothing and carrying a purse, tennis bag, and a bottle of water, enters nervously.

During the scene they talk to each other, but occasionally move their heads to watch the players the audience doesn't see.

RUTHIE

I'm very sorry, Irv. I almost didn't come....

IRV

You're only two minutes late.

RUTHIE

No, I mean sorry about my message.

IRV

What message?

RUTHIE

The text message I left on your phone about an hour ago.

IRV

I don't do texts. What did you say?

RUTHIE

I wrote no, I won't go with you.

IRV

What did I invite you to?

RUTHIE

You invited me to be your doubles partner in
Laughlin.

IRV

Your memory is still good.

RUTHIE

My memory is good and so are my morals, I
want you to know...

IRV

You're forgiven for your morals.

RUTHIE

You never should have asked me. I hope I didn't
hurt your feelings.

IRV

I'll get over it. At 78 you're still worried about
what people will say?

                    RUTHIE
Aren't you?

                      IRV
I'm more worried about my eyesight and how
much longer I can see the ball…and your pretty
face.
            (to the players)
That ball was out!

                    RUTHIE
It was in. Is it macular degeneration?

                      IRV
It's more like total masculine degeneration.

                    RUTHIE
I actually like men who are visually impaired.
They can't see my imperfections. It's harder to
be with someone who can't hear, like Deaf Bill

                      IRV
What did you say? What imperfections?

                    RUTHIE
You need to see an eye doctor, Irv.
You must be blind.

                      IRV
No, just infatuated. Why can't you be my
partner for the tennis weekend?

RUTHIE

I told you why in my text message.

IRV

Which I didn't read. We could drive together
and have separate beds.

RUTHIE

Trudy's going to drive with me. I'd be crazy
driving with a blind person, especially at night.

IRV

We'll go there when it's light. Have
compassion for an old man. Passion would
even be better.

RUTHIE

Stop propositioning me, Irv. I found out you're
married.

IRV

I'm *partially* married. My wife doesn't like to
travel any more, and she doesn't play tennis.

RUTHIE

But I'm sure she doesn't like you taking women
away for the weekend.

IRV

Who's going to tell her?

                    RUTHIE
I'm going to tell her if you don't stop harassing
me.

                    IRV
My wife and I live in the same condo but sleep
in separate rooms. She can't stand my snoring.

                    RUTHIE
I wouldn't be able to either.

                    IRV
I think she just got tired of me. We've been
together a long time. It's better this way. What
about you?

                    RUTHIE
I've had my share of listening to snoring
old men. They all died. It's easier to just
take care of myself now.

                    IRV
All of your parts seem to be working, except
maybe your knees. You look healthy.

                    RUTHIE
I miss dancing.

                    IRV
We could find a place to dance in Laughlin.

RUTHIE

That would be too romantic. Tennis is more
athletic and acceptable.

IRV

I'm glad we can still play tennis.

RUTHIE

My acupuncturist said, "No tennis. Very bad for
knees." I told him I'm not playing Wimbledon.
I'm playing with the old guys. And besides, I
have so much invested in tennis clothes, I can't
give it up.

IRV

That's what I told my doctor. I have so much
invested in condoms and Viagra, I can't give it
up.

RUTHIE

Everything is sex with you. Too bad you're
married.

IRV

Partially married. Listen, at my age, I should be
able to get pleasure and enjoyment wherever I
can. I'm still a good husband and make sure my
wife's car is serviced and the bills are paid and I
help carry in the groceries.

RUTHIE

You're very married and shouldn't flirt with all
the women you meet on the tennis court.

IRV

Never with Trudy. She doesn't appeal to me.

RUTHIE

She's still recovering from hip replacement.

IRV

Won't make a difference. What she needs is voice replacement. That cackle every time she hits a short shot makes me want to throw my racket at her.

RUTHIE

I thought you loved all women, all ages, no matter what they sounded like.

IRV

I love only you right now. Trudy reminds me of my wife, when she's angry at me. What's the score?

RUTHIE

Five-four. Ted and Leah are catching up. I'm glad. Trudy's not as good a player as she thinks she is. I like to play with someone whose balls have pace and speed.

IRV

You're waiting on the wrong court, lady. You're playing with the old guys and their old balls.

RUTHIE

It's just nice being out here in the fresh air.

IRV

There's fresh air in Laughlin too, early in the morning. We could have a wonderful time playing together. It's not as if we'd be alone. Our friends will be there.

RUTHIE

Bill will keep forgetting the score.

IRV

Gary will yell at him to pay attention.

RUTHIE

And you'll be helping the ladies pull down their warm-up pants and getting appreciative hugs.

IRV

Why not take advantage of being an old guy?

RUTHIE

Taking advantage of being an old woman is getting someone to offer you a seat on a bus. This is really a long set.
(takes off jacket)
I'm getting hot flashes.

IRV

Because you're sitting next to me.

RUTHIE

No, because of knee medication.

IRV

Is there any man on the court you'd go to bed with, besides me?

RUTHIE

I'd never go to bed with a married man. What if you had a heart attack?

IRV

I wouldn't abandon you if you had a stroke, or you asked me to rub your knee.

RUTHIE

I'm sorry, Irv. I need a younger man, maybe in his early seventies. See that younger man with the gray hair who just served an ace on court 3?

IRV

My eyesight isn't too good. Does he have on a brown shirt?

RUTHIE

He's not wearing a shirt. Wow! Another ace.

IRV

Do you want to sleep with him or play with him?

RUTHIE

Neither. I just want to watch.

IRV

That's what I find myself doing a lot of these days. I wish Gary would shut up. Those noises are annoying.

RUTHIE

What about Trudy's grunting before each hit? That drives me crazy.

IRV

She's copying Sharapova or having an orgasm.

RUTHIE

Look at those thighs. You'd think she'd be in better shape. Good shot, Trudy. And Gary is diabetic, but still munches on doughnuts at every tournament.

IRV

Don't you have any vices, lady?

RUTHIE

I like a glass of chardonnay occasionally.

IRV

I'd love to buy you a glass of wine in Laughlin next weekend and as many doughnuts as you can eat.

RUTHIE

I told you I don't go out with married men. Read my text.

IRV

It wouldn't be like going out. We could stay
inside the hotel and maybe play a game of
Scrabble or do the slot machines together.

RUTHIE

I think it's a tie breaker. They're almost
finished. Come on, Trudy. Finish them off. I
have a hair appointment in an hour.

IRV

Come on, Gary. An ace serve. I need to take my
wife shopping.

RUTHIE

Forehand or back hand? Which side do you
want?

IRV

The winning side would be fine. Any chance
you'll reconsider my offer?

RUTHIE

No…Well…Maybe coffee and a doughnut after
tennis a week from next Thursday.

IRV

I hope I remember.

RUTHIE

I'll send you a text.

Ruthie walks off waving to Trudy and Bill.

Irv follows behind, frustrated and mumbling.

                    IRV
          But I don't do texts.

Lila Lee Silvern

About the Author

After retiring from a long career as a writer of educational materials for children, Lila Lee Silvern created a new image of herself entertaining at a weekly story salon held at a local coffee house. She was surprised to learn that her young audiences were delighted with her seven minute, ribald stories about seniors still enjoying sex, romance and a good laugh about themselves.

She hoped to inspire the older crowd to drop some of their inhibitions, get more enjoyment out of life after sixty, and give the younger people a more hopeful look at the future. Sensuality after sixty seems to be the last taboo that TV and the movies seem reluctant to explore. This book may embarrass some, but hopefully it will titillate others to drop a few hang ups and grab what's left of their lives with gusto and giggles.

Lila Lee Silvern is a graduate of the UCLA Theatre Arts Department and received a Masters Degree in Bilingual Education from California State University. Northridge. She has had numerous educational materials published and has appeared in a KLCS series called *"The World Comes to Los Angeles."* She is the mother of two sons.

Contact Information

Confessions of a Geriatric Prom Queen

lilaleesilvern@att.net